England's Last Crusader:
Papal Zouave
Giulio Watts-Russell

WITH AN INTRODUCTION BY

FATHER NICHOLAS SCHOFIELD

EDITED BY

BRENDAN CASSELL

Republished By Papal Zouave International
2026

Copyright © Papal Zouave International 2026.

England's Last Crusader: Papal Zouave Giulio Watts-Russell is a republication from Papal Zouave International of *Giulio Watts-Russell, Pontifical Zouave* by Valerian Cardella, S.J., published in 1868 and *Giulio Watts-Russell, Twenty-Seven Years after his Death: A Sequel to his Biography* by Claud R. Lindsay, published in 1895.

For More information regarding this title and Papal Zouave International please visit:

PapalZouave.com

All rights reserved
ISBN: 979-8-9893230-5-0
Cover design by: Brendan Cassell and trieukyquan

Founded in 2023, Papal Zouave International is a historical society dedicated to promoting and preserving the memory of the Papal Zouaves. A unit of brave Catholic soldiers who came from across Christendom to defend the Papal States and Bl. Pope Pius IX during the 9th Crusade, between 1860–1870.

To learn more, visit PapalZouave.com

Contents.

CONTENTS.

Page.

EDITOR'S NOTE i

INTRODUCTION BY FR. SCHOFIELD v

PART I.
BIOGRAPHY OF GIULIO WATTS-RUSSELL

INTRODUCTION BY CARDINAL MANNING 1

CHAPTER I.

Death of Giulio at Mentana—Honours paid to the body in Rome. 3

II.

Arrival of Giulio's Father in Rome 8

III.

Some account of Giulio's life—The happy omen in his baptismal name 14

England's Last Crusader.

IV.

The Mother of Giulio 19

V.

The first years of Giulio in his Family 23

VI.

The years spent by Giulio in College 27

VII.

The last years of Giulio in his Family 32

VIII.

Giulio becomes a Zouave 41

IX.

Giulio's last days and the presentiment of his Death 49

X.

The Day of Sacrafice 58

XI.

Other particulars of Giulio's Death 65

XII.

Marks of esteem and affection shown towards Giulio after death 74

Contents.

XIII.

Giulio's Father 91

GIULIO WATTS-RUSSELL APPENDIX.

Giulio's book of Devotions—A visit to his Tomb 94

PART II.
TWENTY-SEVEN YEARS AFTER HIS DEATH

INTRODUCTION BY LINDSAY 107

CHAPTER I.

The burial of Giulio's Heart in the battle-field of Mentana in 1869—The Monument erected over it—Its destruction by the Garibaldians in 1870—Story of the saving of the Heart and its transmission to England 111

II.

Discovery of Giulio's Monument at Mentana in February, 1894, and the circumstances that led to it—The Monument conveyed to the Church of St. Thomas of Canterbury, at the English College, Rome, and restored 122

England's Last Crusader.

III.

Giulio's grave in the Campo Verano—Exhumation and re-interment of his Remains—Repair of the Grave 140

IV.

The Mentana Letters; also other Letters, recently found, written soon after Giulio's death 152

V.

Monsieur le Chevalier de Geneste—Relics of Giulio found in his possession—Giulio's blood-stained jacket, and Wilfrid's diary of the year 1868—Monsieur de Geneste's letter to myself, June, 1894 171

TWENTY-SEVEN YEARS AFTER HIS DEATH APPENDIX

List of Subscribers to the Fund for the Restoration of Giulio's Grave and Monument... 188

ENGLAND'S LAST CRUSADER APPENDIX

Interview with Julian's Confessor Father Armellini S.J. 191
The Location of Julian's Grave.. 195

Contents.

Julian Watts-Russell in his Parade Uniform

EDITOR'S NOTE.
By Brendan Cassell.

England's Last Crusader: Papal Zouave Giulio Watts-Russell contains two biographies of the English Papal Zouave Julian Watts-Russell.

The first was released a year after his death in 1868, originally written by Valerian Cardella, S.J., a Professor of Dogmatic Theology at the Collegium Romanum (now the Pontifical Gregorian University), who later became a Consultor of the Sacred Congregation of Propaganda. The book, titled *Giulio Watts-Russell, Zuavo Pontificio,* was originally published in Italian for the Roman periodical *Il Divin Salvatore*. That same year, it was translated into English by William Tylee of Oriel College, Oxford, and published by John Philp in London under the title *Giulio Watts-Russell, Pontifical Zouave*.

Twenty-seven years later, in 1895, a sequel incorporating

the previous edition was written by Claud R. Lindsay and published by the Art and Book Company as *Giulio Watts-Russell, Twenty-Seven Years after his Death: A Sequel to his Biography*. The sequel offered additional information and slight corrections, prompted by the discovery of Julian's monument, which now resides at the Venerable English College, and the restoration of his grave at Campo Verano Cemetery in Rome. Lindsay hoped this new edition would expose a fresh generation of Englishmen to the martyrdom and heroism of Julian Watts-Russell.

Now, 131 years later, Papal Zouave International is republishing Lindsay's edition as *England's Last Crusader: Papal Zouave Giulio Watts-Russell*. This edition includes a new introduction by Father Nicholas Schofield, one of England's finest modern historians on the Papal Zouaves and author of *Victorian Crusaders: British and Irish Volunteers in the Papal Army, 1860–70*. Father Schofield's introduction draws on recent research to offer fresh insight into the life and story of Julian Watts-Russell, enriching the narrative beyond what was available to either Cardella or Lindsay. Unlike previous republished editions from Papal Zouave International, this edition retains the original British spellings and grammatical style, which seemed more fitting for a book about an Englishman.

This edition also contains a map of Campo Verano Cemetery in Rome, tracing a path from the entrance to the monument dedicated to the Papal soldiers who fell in 1867 fighting in defence of the Papal States against Garibaldi

Editor's Note.

and his Red Shirts, the same conflict in which Julian was martyred. The monument features a relief of St. Peter gifting a sword to a Crusader and bears the names of all the Papal soldiers who died in the 1867 campaign, Julian Watts-Russell among them. Nearby lie the graves of many other Papal Zouave heroes alongside whom Julian is buried.

Unfortunately, over the past 131 years, the exact location of his grave has been lost. However, it is believed to lie just behind the 1867 campaign monument, against the cemetery wall by the road. Once the grave is rediscovered, a future edition of this book will contain a map to Julian's final resting place.

The principal purpose of this republication is the same as it was for Lindsay's sequel in 1895: to introduce the sacrifice and martyrdom of Julian Watts-Russell to a new generation of Englishmen and the wider Christian world, so that his sacrifice may be remembered and his piety emulated. Perhaps one day he will be raised to the altar, as so many of his comrades believed he would be. Perhaps not. Either way, Julian, like so many other Papal Zouaves, embodied the virtues of faith, hope, and charity. For that reason alone, his memory ought to be preserved.

INTRODUCTION.
By Father Nicholas Schofield.

THE Venerable English College, situated in the heart of Rome is the oldest English institution overseas still in existence. It was founded as a seminary in 1579 on the site of a medieval pilgrim hospice and its chapel, though only dating to the 1880s, is full of historical associations and monuments. Its arrangement and decoration was not only intended to constitute a 'national' church for English Catholics in the Eternal City but also to celebrate the long tradition of British martyrs. Their sufferings, stretching back to the early centuries of the Church, are depicted in often gruesome detail in the frescoes found in the Tribune. Above the main altar is the impressive 'Martyrs' Picture' by Durante Alberti (1538-1613), depicting the Holy Trinity with St Edmund, the martyred King of East Anglia, and St Thomas of Canterbury, famously murdered in his cathedral in 1170. It was before this image that the *Te Deum* was sung whenever news reached the College that one of their alumni had been put to death in Elizabethan and Stuart England. There were 44 priest martyrs in all, starting with St Ralph Sherwin in 1581. St Thomas himself, the original patron of the pilgrim hospice, was rediscovered in the nineteenth century as a martyr for the freedom and unity of the Church against an aggressive secular power.[1]

At the back of the chapel is a monument that is easily missed, especially since it is beside the entrance, and was only brought to the College in 1894; nevertheless, it forms part of this 'visual martyrology.' It is cylindrical in shape, with a cross, and bears the name of Julian Watts-Russell (1850-67), a Pontifical Zouave who was killed at the battle of Mentana, aged seventeen and ten months, while defending the pope's temporal sovereignty. He was the youngest to fall that day and the nearest to the town, which was then occupied by Garibaldi. He came from a wealthy English family yet spent much of his short life in Italy, France, Germany and Corsica; one aunt was married to an Italian baron and another to the son of a prominent Bavarian minister.[2] The fact that his relatives and friends called him 'Giulio' rather than 'Julian', as we shall do, is testament to this European background.

This volume contains two important accounts of Giulio's life, death and subsequent cultus: a biography by the Jesuit Valerian Cardella (1820-91), originally written shortly after his death, and a 'sequel' dating from 27 years later by Claud

---

[1] See Nicholas Schofield, 'St Thomas Becket (c. 1118-1170): Patron of the Venerable English College Church, Rome, and of the English Clergy' in Maurice Whitehead (ed), *Memory, Martyrs, and Mission: Essays to Commemorate the 850th Anniversary of the Martyrdom of St Thomas Becket (c.1118-1170)* (Rome: Gangemi Editore, 2020)

[2] Baron de Martini (previously military commendant at Milan) and Count de Montgelas.

Introduction by Fr. Schofield.

R. Lindsay (1861-1918), an English cleric based in Rome, describing an attempt to revive interest in the Zouave.³

Tellingly, there is a 'Preface', written in 1868 for Cardella's memoir, by the Archbishop of Westminster, Henry Edward Manning (1808-92), who would become one of the leading ultramontane voices at the First Vatican Council. He recalls meeting Giulio and his brother, Wilfrid (1846-79) on the Piazza Farnese in July 1867; this was presumably while the Archbishop was staying at the English College, situated in an adjoining street, during the celebrations of the 18th Centenary of St Peter's Martyrdom – an opportunity used by Pius IX (1792-1878) to stress the authority of the Papacy, the unity and vibrancy of the Church and the transnational nature of its membership at a time of crisis. If this event was a 'spectacle' to the world, contrasting with the Universal Exposition in Paris that same year, then Giulio would shortly become part of its manifestation: 'if it be true that...the cause makes the martyr,' writes Manning, 'this noble disciple and soldier of Jesus Christ has won a martyr's crown.' In the monumental scheme of the English College chapel, Giulio takes his place in a long procession of British martyrs who shed their blood for Christ, the Church and the See of Peter.

Giulio is presented in these pages as a model Zouave and an example for Catholic youth, mixing deep piety with heroic courage; indeed, before his birth a 'holy nun' had prayed that

---

3   For more recent accounts, see Richard Whinder, 'Julian Watts-Russell and the Papal Zouaves' in Nicholas Schofield (ed), *A Roman Miscellany:* The English in Rome 1550-2000 (Leominster: Gracewing, 2002), and Nicholas Schofield, *Victorian Crusaders: British and Irish Volunteers in the Papal Army 1860-70* (Warwick: Helion, 2022).

he would obtain 'the necessary qualities to combat victoriously the enemies of our holy religion.' There is a stress on his readiness to seek forgiveness, his zeal for the Catholic Faith (even to the extent of contemplating a missionary life in Australia), his book of personal prayers (the line *'Anima mia, anima mia, Ama Dio e tira via'* became the motto of the Canadian Zouaves), and his love for his older brother and fellow Zouave, to whom the book was dedicated.

Cardella's memoir is an expansion of a series of articles written within weeks of Giulio's death for *Il Divin Salvatore*, a Catholic weekly printed in Rome.[4] Its author was a prominent Jesuit in the city. He taught dogmatic theology at the Roman College and, shortly after the publication of this volume, became its Rector; he was later appointed Roman Provincial and Consultor to the Sacred Congregation of Propaganda (now the Dicastery for Evangelisation). He was considered an authoritative theologian, with access to the Vatican at its highest levels, and had under his influence *La Civiltà Cattolica*, one of the leading ultramontane periodicals of the time, with a wide readership; it was often considered the unofficial mouthpiece of the Holy See.

Despite these Roman credentials, Cardella had a keen interest in Great Britain. During the upheavals of 1848-49 he had left the Eternal City for the safety of north Wales and the newly founded St Beuno's College. Alongside his teaching duties, he 'charitably devoted his leisure hours to assisting the poor Catholics of St Asaph,' with the help of Colonel and

---

4   *Il Divin Salvatore*, 16 November 1867, pp109-110; 23 November 1867, p120; 28 December 1867, pp205-07; 4 January 1868, pp214-16.

Introduction by Fr. Schofield. ix

Mrs Nicholas Blundell, a prominent Catholic couple then living in the area.[5] Returning to Rome, Cardella kept alive his Anglophone connections, acting as confessor to visitors and residents alike: thus, he received the noted American landscape painter, George L. Browne, into the Church (1858) and ministered to Major-General Tylee, a convert who was formerly of the Indian Army, on his deathbed (1865). He acted as spiritual director and friend of Giulio's father and came to know his sons after they moved to Rome in 1863.

Cardella's biography was translated from the Italian by William Tylee (1837-1911), a cousin of the aforementioned General, who had been educated at Oriel College, Oxford, and briefly at Cuddesdon, the Anglican theological college, before becoming a Catholic in 1866. He studied for the Priesthood at St Mary's College, Oscott and in Rome, and was ordained for the Archdiocese of Westminster in 1868. After a period at the Pro-Cathedral in Kensington, he became chaplain to the Marquess of Ripon and spent a period in India; by this time he had gained the title of monsignor. It was during his brief stay as a student in Rome that he met Giulio.

There are some notable omissions from the narrative. Cardella includes a chapter on the sanctity of Giulio's mother, Augusta (1813-51), who died while he was still an infant;— indeed, contemporary accounts of Zouaves often focused on the piety and self-sacrifice of the mother. However, Cardella says little of the Watts-Russell family, beyond mentioning that their seat was at Ilam Hall on

---

5   Henry Foley SJ, *Records of the English Province of the Society of Jesus*, vol. 5 (London: Burns and Oates, 1878), p945

the Staffordshire-Derbyshire border.

Who, then, were the Watts-Russells? Often presented as a successful parvenu Victorian family, the name was only created by Royal Licence in 1817 after Jesse Russell (1786-1875) married Mary Watts (1792-1840), daughter and heiress of David Pike Watts (1754-1816), a wealthy wine merchant. It has been claimed that the family had humble beginnings and were dismissed by some of their peers as *nouveau riche*, Jesse's father being a 'soap boiler' of Goodman's Yard, The Minories in the City of London.[6] However, the Russells were a well-established Staffordshire gentry family, claiming distant descent from the Russell Earls and Dukes of Bedford.[7] Jesse Russell Senior (1743-1820) converted a glasshouse, which had produced bottles, into a successful soap and tallow factory.[8] With the profits, he had been able to purchase a large property in Walthamstow (Essex) and send his son to Eton College and Worcester College, Oxford. He was a Livery Man of the Carpenters' and Joiners' Company and involved in various charitable works.

By 1820 the fathers of both Jesse and Mary had died and the couple enjoyed a vast inheritance. They rebuilt Ilam

---

6   See for example the official Parliamentary biography www.histparl.ac.uk/volume/1820-32/member/watts-russell-jesse-1786-1875 (accessed 19 November 2025) or *Derby and Chesterfield Reporter*, 29 March 1912, p4: he 'made a vast fortune as a soap boiler in London.'

7   Gordon Nares, 'Biggin Hall, Northamptonshire' in Country Life, 18 November 1954, p1758. It is ironic that Giulio, who died in defence of the pope's temporal sovereignty, could claim connection to Lord John Russell, a two-times Prime Minister who, as Foreign Secretary, was a prominent supporter of Italian Unification.

8   London Archives: City of London, MS 11936/360/555497, Insurance Certificate for Jesse Russell, Soap Manufacturer, 23 March 1789.

Hall, which Mary's father had purchased in 1809, in the neo-gothic style. The house boasted a long picture gallery with fine models of the ruins of Rome, which must have fired Wilfrid and Giulio's imagination. An auction of some of its contents arranged by one of Jesse's sons in 1875 included paintings by Lely, Constable, Gainsborough and Turner, and a fine library, giving an insight into its splendour.[9] The surroundings were stunningly beautiful; the topographer Ebenezer Rhodes (1762-1839) thought that 'no glen in the Alps was ever more retired, or more delightful to behold' and that in visiting Ilam 'I felt as if I were treading on fairy ground.' [10]The scenery inspired Dr Samuel Johnson (1709-84) to write his description of 'Happy Valley' in *The History of Rasselas, Prince of Abissinia* (1759), and the playwright William Congreve (1670-1729) also wrote some of his works there.[11]

In 1822 the Watts-Russells acquired Biggin Hall (Northamptonshire), an estate that had once belonged to the Abbots of Peterborough and (briefly) Queen Katherine Parr (1512-48), Henry VIII's sixth wife. Jesse went on to serve as High Sheriff of Staffordshire and Member of Parliament for the rotten borough of Gatton, near Reigate (1820-26), which by the time of its abolition in 1832 returned two MPs despite having only seven qualified voters.[12] After his death, Jesse

---

9 The artist John Constable (1776-1837) was the nephew of David Pike Watts and therefore Giulio's first cousin twice removed.
10 Ebenezer Rhodes, The Derbyshire Tourist (London, 1824), p.330
11 The Ilam estate was bequeathed to the National Trust in 1934; the house is now a youth hostel.
12 He unsuccessfully tried for election as the Member for North Staffordshire and was presented by his grateful supporters with a four feet high silver candelabra

was remembered as 'one of the few remaining Parliamentary veterans who sat in the unreformed House of Commons in the time of George IV, and was altogether a fine specimen of the true country gentleman.'[13] He 'used to wear a complete suit of sealskin-trousers, vest and coat, and all lined with the best of silk.'[14]

Jesse took his responsibilities as a landowner seriously. The churches of Holy Cross, Ilam and St Mary the Virgin, Benefield were rebuilt, the former acquiring a large neo-gothic mausoleum for David Pike Watts.[15] Ilam itself was transformed into a model village, with new school buildings and houses in the Swiss style, and a large monument, inspired by the Eleanor Cross, erected after Mary's death in 1840.

The church at Benefield is a superb example of the early Gothic Revival, based on Tractarian principles and subsequently embellished by Sir Ninian Comper (1864-1960). Its spire is a prominent local landmark.

Jesse appointed Rev. John Miller (1787-1858) as Rector in 1825, admired by many as a conscientious pastor and gifted preacher, and a close friend of John Keble (1792-1866). In 1842 Miller was replaced by Jesse's second son and Giulio's father, Michael (1815-75); the same year he married Augusta Barker. Michael had been educated at Eton,

---

in August 1834.
13 *Derby Mercury*, 7 April 1875, p5
14 *Derby and Chesterfield Reporter*, 29 March 1912, p4
15 Despite its Victorian make-over, Holy Cross dates back to Saxon times and claimed the tomb of St Bertram (Beorhthelm, Bertelin, or Bettelin), an obscure Mercian prince who became a hermit in the eighth century.

Introduction by Fr. Schofield. xiii

St. Mary the Virgin in Benefield and the Watts-Russell coat of arms inside.

like his father, and Christ Church, Oxford, where he became influenced by the Oxford Movement and in particular St John Henry Newman (1801-90), proclaimed by Leo XIV as a Doctor of the Church. Ordained as an Anglican priest for the Diocese of Peterborough in 1842, Michael quickly put his Catholicising ideals into practice at Benefield, celebrating Holy Communion each Sunday and Morning and Evening Prayer daily. He was encouraged in this by Frederick William Faber (1814-63), Rector of nearby Elton, who won fame as an author, hymnwriter and founder of the London Oratory.

Cardella speaks of the close connection of the Watts-Russells with Faber: the young Giulio could frequently be found at the Oratory church and at the Fathers' country residence at Sydenham (Surrey), living 'under the shadow of St Philip [Neri].' However, no mention is made of Newman, who not only inspired the young Michael but corresponded with him. [16] By the time Cardella's memoir was published, Newman was a controversial figure in Rome. He had long been under a cloud of suspicion, especially after his 1859 article 'On Consulting the Faithful in Matters of Doctrine' which some thought contained material heresy, and his plans to establish an Oratory at Oxford and thus bring Catholics to the University had recently been defeated. Despite being closely allied to the ultramontane party, Cardella was sympathetic to Newman. In March 1867 he had invited Newman to contribute to an 'album' of articles on St Peter that would

---

16   Newman quickly wrote to Michael informing him of his conversion. In December 1847 the future cardinal sent Augusta, Giulio's mother, a crucifix blessed at Loreto.

be presented to the pope. Newman accepted but was wary; he noted in a letter that the Roman Jesuits and *La Civiltà Cattolica* were generally against the Oxford Oratory project. Despite his apparent friendliness, Newman thought 'Father Cardella has two faces.'[17] When Ambrose St John travelled to Rome soon afterwards in Newman's defence, Cardella offered some assistance, albeit discreetly - 'he said we must keep peace with our own people, though I wish to serve Fr. N. [Newman] in any way in my power.'[18] It seems probable that Cardella purposefully omitted reference to Newman so as not to distract from the main message of the memoir.

Despite the rebuilding of Benefield church, Jesse did not share the Tractarian sympathies of his second son and was generally suspicious of Catholics. Indeed, as MP he had voted against measures for Catholic Relief and in 1843 prominently supported the erection of a memorial to the Protestant Martyrs in Oxford (1843), which was designed to assert the Protestant nature of the Church of England and counter the Oxford Movement. In 1845 both Newman and Faber became Catholic. Michael and his young family followed suit. This was no easy decision, for it meant they were written out of Jesse's will, which stated:

> if any child of the said Michael W. Watts Russell shall... take Orders in the Church of Rome, or become a professed member of the Church of Rome, or enter as a novice in any

---

17   C. S. Dessain & T. Gosnell (ed), *The Letters and Diaries of John Henry Newman*, vol. 23 (Oxford: Clarendon Press, 1973), p.112
18   *Ibid.*, p. 225; see also Joseph Carola SJ, 'Newman and the Roman College: A Formative Exchange' in *Nova et Vetera* (English edition) Vol. 18, No. 3, p.755

religious community belonging to the Church of Rome, or shall at my death be in such Orders, or be such professed member or such novice, as aforesaid, then and in every case, every such child shall in the construction of the above bequest be deemed to have died without issue in my lifetime.[19]

Nevertheless, relations were not completely broken: the Watts-Russell brothers were at Ilam Hall in the second half of 1866 and the beginning of 1867, leading, as can be imagined, 'a very pleasant life' and 'earning always more and more the affection of their grandfather and Mrs Watts-Russell.'[20] During this stay, Giulio's brother, Michael (1848-1912) left to join the Passionist novitiate at Broadway, though he was nearly killed in a game involving a loaded musket that had long hung on the walls of Ilam.

The young Giulio possessed all the masculine qualities that were expected in the mid-nineteenth century. Indeed, as a student briefly at St Cuthbert's College, Ushaw (1861-63), the Catholic school and seminary near Durham, 'he was so fond of amusement and bold adventures that he not unfrequently got into "scrapes"' and was particularly influenced by nautical tales. He wrote a story in which he himself

---

19   Transcription sent to the author by Dr Julian Watts-Russell, 20 May 2021. It is interesting that in 1879 Michael's older brother, Jesse David (1812-79), built a second Anglican church in Oundle, a town near Benefield, dedicated to the Holy Name of Jesus,. In 1971 it was sold to the Catholic Diocese of Northampton and still serves as the local Catholic parish church.
20   Jesse was widowed in 1840 and three years later married Maria Ellen Barker (1818-44), who was (extraordinarily) the younger sister of Giulio's mother, Augusta (his daughter-in-law). She died shortly afterwards and in 1862 he married for the third time, to Martha Leech (1842-1917), later Mrs Lodge.

Introduction by Fr. Schofield. xvii

Ilam Hall.

sailing to Australia in a little boat and on one occasion escaped the college, with a companion, turning their coats inside out as disguise and carrying only two shillings between them. They hoped to reach the nearest seaport and embark on 'some strange adventure' but lost their way and were brought back to the college, tired and hungry. After news of his death reached his alma mater, it was proudly said that Giulio ran away from Ushaw but did not fly before the muskets at Mentana.

Wilfrid and Giulio were among the first English volunteers to join the Pontifical Zouaves in defence of the pope, enlisting on 1 June 1867 (matriculation numbers 4101 and 4102).[21] The regiment had been established at the start of 1861, based on the remnant of an earlier unit, the Franco-Belgian Tirailleurs, which had seen distinguished action against the Piedmontese the previous year. One of this remnant seems to have been of English birth: Joseph (or Charles) Wells of London, though he had left the Zouaves by July 1861.

It was not until the crisis of 1867 that the Zouaves became substantially more international in nature. Two English Zoauves lost their lives in the 1867 campaign: Alfred Collingridge (1846-67), during the action at Montelibretti, and Giulio, and their example led to renewed interest and an avalanche of enlistments from across the Channel. Significantly, it seems that the Collingridges and Watts-Russells came to know about the Zouaves through their

---

21   Wilfrid left the Zouaves on 21 September 1867 and rejoined on 21 August 1870 (no. 10694) for the final assault in Rome. He died on 11 October 1879, at which time he was living at 16 Liston Road, Wandsworth, London.

Introduction by Fr. Schofield.

continental connections. Alfred Collingridge had recently left the Institute Notre Dame in Auteuil, on the outskirts of Paris, while the Watts-Russells, as we have seen, led a peripatetic existence around Europe. Moreover, both were considering a priestly vocation, potentially with the Society of Jesus; becoming a priest and a Zouave were seen as closely connected, giving service to the Church at a time of peril.[22]

The Watts-Russell brothers had considered joining the Austrian army during the war of 1866 but were discouraged by the Foreign Enlistment Act of 1819, which prevented British subjects from serving under a foreign flag. It seems they had undertaken some training in Graz and Munich, which proved useful in Rome. Giulio's service with the Zouaves was initially uneventful and Cardella speaks of the 'noble daily sacrifice of the laborious and humble life of the private soldier.' There was also a strong religious dimension; the Zouaves by Cardella are presented as a new military order and Giulio, like many of his comrades, was conscientious in visiting churches, celebrating the sacraments, and seeking perfection. Tellingly there is a reference to Zouaves touching their rosary beads and bayonets to holy relics; both were seen as weapons in the spiritual combat at hand.

Giulio's service with the Zouaves was cut short by his death on the battlefield of Mentana on 3 November 1867. Shot through the right eye, he would have died immedi-

---

[22] Cardella confessed to having hopes that Giulio would become a Jesuit. When Jeremiah Crowley prepared to set off for the Zouaves in the spring of 1869, Archbishop Manning met him and remarked 'to be a soldier for the Pope was the next best thing to being a priest' (The Tablet, 5 June 1869, p.20).

ately; according to one unverified report, his killer was an English Garibaldian who was 'a crack shot and delighted in shooting his victims in the eye from the window of a town house.'[23] The young Zouave was immediately venerated as a martyr, his body being carefully moved from the cemetery at Monte Rotondo to Rome, where it was embalmed and laid out for three days in a house near the basilica of Santa Maria Maggiore. The Requiem was celebrated at the chapel of the English College[24] and the coffin then taken for burial at Campo Verano.

It has been noted that martyrs were an important element of nineteenth century Catholicism and closely linked to the campaign to defend and promote the authority of the pope. Martyr cults included those in the distant past – as seen in the renewed interest in the martyrs of the early Church and the removal of their relics from the Roman catacombs and distribution across the world, thanks to the archaeological discoveries of Giovanni Battista de Rossi (1822-94) - as well as those in the nineteenth century. According to Lucy Riall, 'Zouave martyrs were both warrior heroes and devoutly religious, and fighting for the pope became one way for a young man to take part in the Catholic revival and follow the martyr's path to holiness.'[25] Just like the early Roman

---

23   *The Tablet*, 17 March 1894, p.415 (the testimony of Giulio's confessor, Fr Armellini).
24   Not the current chapel, which only dates from 1888, but presumably the Martyrs' Chapel, opposite the refectory, which was used for services for much of the nineteenth century. The old college chapel had to be rebuilt due to the devastation of the Napoleonic occupation.
25   Lucy Riall, 'Martyr Cults in Nineteenth Century Italy' in *Journal of Modern History*, vol. 82, no. 2 (June 2010), p.285

Introduction by Fr. Schofield. xxi

martyrs, they were presented as models of purity and piety. Secular cults also existed around those who died for the nationalist cause, informed by the sentimentalism that was prevalent at the time and likewise promoted by affordable publications and images.

Giulio's cult is vividly described in these pages. – We read of the devotees praying in front of his body that reportedly remained fresh and supple, the palms of martyrdom placed around him, the flowers on his grave taken from the pope's garden, the presence of his fellow Zouaves and friends from England, descriptions of him as an 'angel' and a 'child crusader.' There was interest in Giulio, of course, in his homeland, as witnessed by the English translation of Cardella's memoir and the distribution of his image at Ushaw, but what is striking is the transnational dimension of the cult. As we have seen, Cardella wrote accounts of Giulio's life in popular Roman publications within weeks of his death. His memoir was republished by request of the bishop of Ajaccio and widely distributed around Corsica. A sermon preached on Giulio at the Bavarian church of Egglkofen that Christmas produced marvellous results; his aunt, the Countess de Montgelas, had a house nearby, and Giulio and Wilfrid spent time there before joining the Zouaves and engaged in an apostolate with the peasants.

It is interesting that Alfred Collingridge, the other English martyr of 1867, did not attract such a cultus. He had much in common with Giulio, coming from a well-connected family, showing great piety and expressing admirable sentiments on his deathbed: 'The Lord has given me the favour I asked – to die for the Holy Father. Oh yes, may God accept of my death and my blood for the triumph of the Holy Church and for the conversion of England.'[26] However, he did not have the extent of Giulio's international connections and supporters, meaning that it was Giulio not Alfred who could stand alongside the other papal martyrs of the 1860s and be proclaimed as the Guérin of England.[27]

The second half of this volume contains a 'sequel' by Claud Reginald Lindsay (1861-1918) giving further evidence of Giulio's cult. Lindsay was educated at Beaumont, Stonyhurst and the elite Accademia Ecclesiastica in Rome, and boasted two earls as grandfathers.[28] Ordained in 1895 and named a monsignor three years later, he was for many years attached to the Roman church of San Silvestro in Capite, before retiring to South Kensington.[29] While preparing for ordination he attempted to revive interest in Giulio, especially by safeguarding the relic of his heart, buried on the battlefield of Mentana in 1869,[30] and its accompanying monument, which was moved to the English College. The Zouave's body was also exhumed and his tomb restored. Those involved in the scheme included the Servant of God Rafael Merry del Val (1865-1930), an alumnus of Ushaw, who went on to become the Cardinal Secretary of State under St Pius X, and

---

26   *The Tablet*, 26 October 1867, p.681
27   Louis-Joseph Guérin (1838-60) was killed at the battle of Castelfidardo and had a similar reputation for sanctity.
28   24th Earl of Crawford and 4th Earl of Wicklow.
29   *Tablet*, 27 July 1918, p.95
30   This was in the presence of his father, who had recently been ordained a Catholic priest. He worked for many years at the shrine of Lourdes.

Introduction by Fr. Schofield. xxiii

his contemporary Arthur Hinsley (1865-1943), also a former Ushaw student, who later became Rector of the English College and Cardinal Archbishop of Westminster.

Giulio's heart was eventually sent to the Darlington Carmel, where Giulio was well known[31] and where his sister Catherine (1843-1917) was a member of the community (Sister Maria Julian of Our Lady of Lourdes). The casket was buried near the altar of Our Lady in the nuns' choir until being removed during reordering in 1971 and placed in the grave of his sister in the Carmel's cemetery.[32]

Unfortunately, Lindsay's hopes of reviving Giulio's cult were ultimately unsuccessful. There are only occasional references to Giulio after 1895; in 1913, for example, he was presented as a model of 'discipline, decency and devotion' to the Catholic Boys' Brigade at St Joseph's, Longsight (Manchester).[33] There was no cause for beatification and no further publications, beyond the occasional mention in the in-house journals of Ushaw and the Venerable English College. Few modern visitors notice his monument at Campo Verano.

---

31   Giulio had stayed with the chaplain, Fr Joseph Brown (1794-1877), a well-known and zealous priest and scholar, who had been Rector of the Royal English College, Valladolid (Spain).
32   Email to the author by Margaret Harcourt-Williams, who was cataloguing the papers of the Darlington Carmel kept at Douai Abbey, 28 June 2022. The Carmel traced its origins to the foundation of a community of English Carmelite nuns at Lierre (Belgium) in 1648. In 2010 the community was forced to move to smaller premises due to dwindling numbers. At the time of closure, the Northen Echo of 14 September 2010 reported that 'one of the deceased sisters was buried with the pickled heart of her brother, killed in battle.' The nun's cemetery remains, the stone crosses bearing only the nuns' initials and the year of their deaths.
33   The Monitor and New Era, 22 March 1913, p.13

Nevertheless, the republication of this rare volume is most welcome. It is an important resource in the history of the British volunteers who joined the pope's army in the 1860s and gives a fascinating insight into the life of a wealthy and notable mid-Victorian convert family. It is both a biography of Giulio and one of the principal engines behind his cultus, itself forming part of the story. Written by a Roman Jesuit and translated from Italian, Cardella's biography is a reminder of the international nature of the volunteer movement, while Lindsay's sequel shows the enduring power of martyrdom in the life of the Church. The piety and example of this young Zouave, despite his quintessentially English background, was as relevant for the readers in Corsica, Germany or Canada as it was for his fellow countrymen.

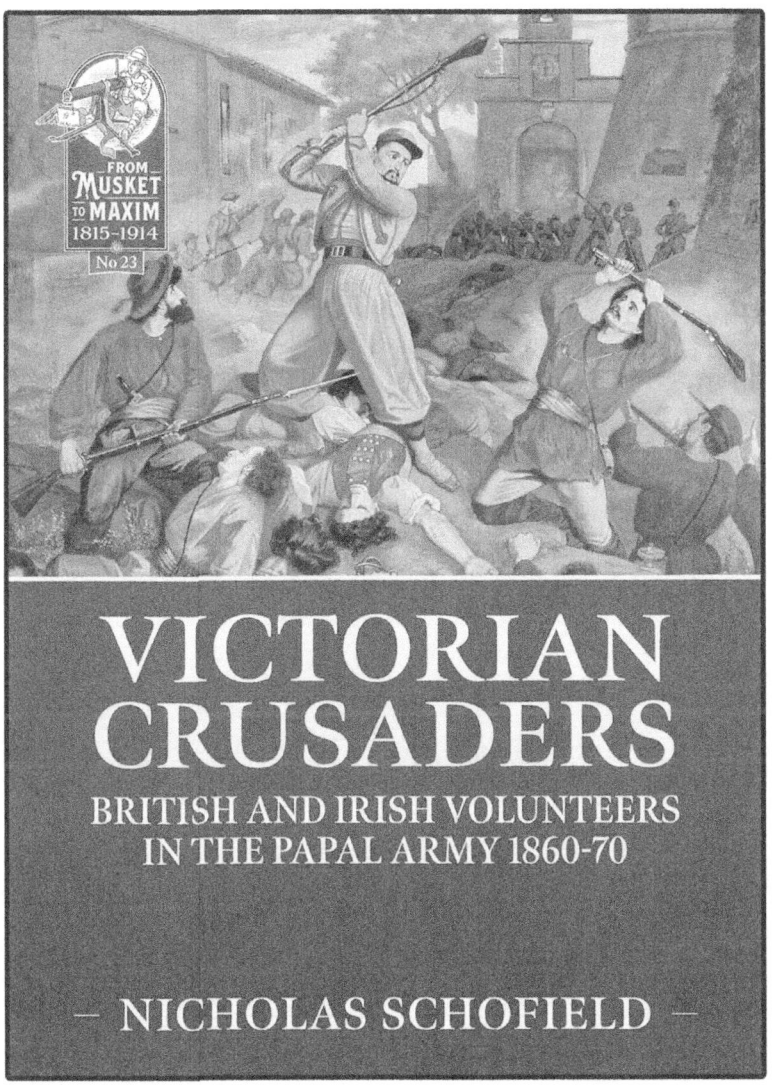

To Learn more about the English Papal Zouaves, check out the book:
Victorian Crusaders: British and Irish Volunteers in the Papal Army 1860-1870
by Father Nicholas Schofield

GIULIO WATTS-RUSSELL
PONTIFICAL ZOUAVE

BY THE LATE

MOST REV. VALERIAN CARDELLA, S.J.

Consultor of the Sacred Congregation of the Propaganda

TRANSLATED FROM THE ITALIAN BY

MONSIGNOR WILLIAM TYLEE, M.A.

Oriel College, Oxford

WITH A PREFACE BY THE LATE

CARDINAL MANNING

ORIGINALLY PUBLISHED IN 1868 BY

LONDON:
JOHN PHILP, 7, ORCHARD STREET,
PORTMAN SQUARE.

DEDICATED
TO WILFRID,
GIULIO'S BROTHER.

Wilfrid Watts-Russell

Cardinal Edward Manning

THE following narrative of a heroic death, in defence of the Vicar of Jesus Christ, is so touching and beautiful, that I heartily commend it to the faithful, especially to our youth in England, without any words of my own. I remember bidding farewell to Julian and Wilfrid Watts-Russell, in their Zouave uniform, on the Piazza Farnese in July last year. I little thought then of the duty of veneration I am fulfilling now. If it be true that *"Causa facit martyrem,"* the cause makes the martyr, this noble disciple and soldier of Jesus Christ has won a martyr's crown. May thousands arise and fill his place, and may at least their life be like his.

HENRY EDWARD,
Archbishop of Westminster.

October 23rd, 1868.

The Battle of Mentana by Lionel Royer

CHAPTER I.

Death of Giulio[1] at Mentana. Honours paid to the body in Rome.

AMONG the glorious victims of Mentana, one of the most renowned was the young Pontifical Zouave, Giulio Watts-Russell, of the English Family of Watts-Russell, of Ilam Hall, near Ashbourne, Staffordshire; who died on the field of battle, on the third of November, 1867, at the age of seventeen years and nine months.

Five months before the battle, Giulio, together with his elder brother Wilfrid, had generously enlisted among the Zouaves as a private soldier. He fought bravely at Nerola, side by side with his brother; and from thence he went to Monte Rotondo, leaving the latter at Rome, laid up with a fever, occasioned by the fatigues of the campaign; and therefore forbidden by the commanding officer to accompany his regiment to Mentana. Before they parted, they recited the *Pater*, *Ave* and *Salve* together, and shook hands, and Giulio, armed

---

1   His real name was Julian, but as he was always called among his relatives by the Italian equivalent, it has been thought better to retain it inthis translation.

and with his knapsack on his shoulder, took his place in the ranks. It was the first time that they had been separated; and, before twenty-four hours had passed, the noble youth had the happiness which he so long desired of shedding his blood *"pro Sede Petri."*

The day before, according to his custom, he had been fortified with the holy Sacraments, and, as his companions testified, "spoke little but prayed much." Almost at the very beginning of the battle he lost his cap, which was struck off by a ball. On several occasions he ran considerable risk; and at last, near Mentana, he fell, struck by a ball, which pierced the right eye and entered the brain; and he lay stretched on the ground, not far from a Garibaldian.

Mrs. Stone, who, with three Sisters of Charity, found him on the field, begged that the body might be put aside, and not placed amongst the others, in order that it might be conveyed, together with the account of his death, to his brother in Rome. A little manuscript book of devotion was found on the body, and at the end of it were these lines, written in Italian, which will express his pious, frank, and noble character:—

"Anima mia, anima mia
Ama Dio e tira via."[2]

Besides which, there is a prayer, in French, to the most Blessed Virgin, entreating for the conversion of those who, even in the midst of their sins, had preserved one spark of

---

[2] My soul, my soul, be this thy song,
Love thy God, and speed along.

devotion to her. And who knows whether the conversion of some of the wounded Garibaldians was not owing to such prayers as these? The whole book is a jewel of devotion, which manifests the fervent piety of the young Zouave. He was beloved by all for his innocent habits and generosity of heart. To understand his beautiful character it will be enough to mention that, a short time before these events, he had had a little difference with his brother on some trifling matter, which Giulio interrupted by saying, "Wilfrid, let us kneel down and make an act of contrition and then shake hands." And so they did, and thus ended their short *"amantium ira."*

They are well able to be brave soldiers who thus know how to conquer themselves.

A French gentleman who had been Giulio's friend, assisted by a French priest, brought the body from Mentana to Rome, and it was embalmed in the house of the same gentleman. He it was who had the good fortune to take care of, and to send to France, the body of the Zouave Guerin, after the battle of Castelfidardo; and I might well say that the young Watts-Russell is the Guerin of England.

As soon as the body was laid out in the house, a wreath of white roses was placed upon it, with a crucifix, and the palm of martyrdom; and around the neck the scapular of Mary. And so it remained for several days, during which time many people came to see it; and as they gazed on the calm and beautiful countenance, they exclaimed, "What an angel he looks." It was a touching spectacle—this noble boy, in his Zouave uniform, with a sweet smile, which was almost supernatural, lying in graceful attitude, as if he were asleep.

The blood-stained uniform which Giulio wore on the battle-field, was preserved for the consolation of his father (a father worthy indeed of such a son), as a family relic.

On the evening of Friday, the 9th of November, the body was brought to the English College in a funeral car, and was received processionally at the door by all the students and the new Rector, Father O'Callaghan, of the Oblates of S. Charles, in London; and on Saturday morning the Office and Mass were sung in its presence. Monsignor Talbot, Mgr. Stonor, and several English gentlemen and ladies, as well as some of the Zouaves who had been Giulio's companions, were present; and it was a beautiful sight to see the latter assisting at the Mass and Absolutions, with their rosaries and lighted candles in their hands. Among them we remarked two Zouaves, Cary and Collingridge; the first of these was Giulio's companion in battle at his last moments; the other the cousin of Cary, and the brother of that brave man who, having been mortally wounded at Monte Libretti, was the first among the English who had the honour to die for so holy a cause. The predominant feeling was one of tender consolation and holy envy for the dead; and although until now Wilfrid had felt to the quick his brother's death, in the end he could not help saying that "the funeral had left upon him the impression of a *'Festa.'*"

The wonder and the consolation of those around was renewed when, for the last time, they uncovered the body, before placing it in its leaden coffin. That sweet smile on the innocent face, and that suppleness of the whole body, assured them that he slept the sleep of peace.

Towards evening he was carried to the place which had been prepared in the Cemetery of S. Lorenzo, outside the walls; and his brother laid upon his tomb two wreaths of flowers gathered in the Pope's own garden, praying for peace to the soul of his dearest Giulio, who, we hope, already had his crown and palm in Heaven.

I will end this chapter with the inscription which I have written on the monument.

HEIC AD MARTYRUM CRYPTAS
DORMIT IN PACE
JULIANUS WATTS-RUSSELL MICHAELIS F.
ANGLUS CLARO GENERE
PRO PETRI SEDE STRENUE DIMICANS
IN ACIE AD NOMENTUM OCCUBUIT
III NON NOVEMB. AN. MDCCCLXVII.
AN. N. XVII. MENS X
ADOLESCENS CHRISTI MILES
VIVE IN DEO.

CHAPTER II.

Arrival of Giulio's Father in Rome.

ONE week after the funeral, Mr. Michael Watts-Russell unexpectedly arrived in Rome, having only just heard of his son's death. When I saw him I gave him my hand, and said, "I do not know whether I ought first to condole with the Father or congratulate the Christian." And he, taking my hand, after a moment's silence, answered, "I am satisfied." Then, after a short pause, he added, "If I had ten sons I would willingly sacrifice them to God for a cause so holy." I had, indeed, written to him at Saragossa, where he had been, with his daughter, on a devout pilgrimage to the Sanctuary of *Our Lady of the Pillar*; but the letters had not reached him in time; and he saw the notice of Giulio's death at Marseilles while reading an article in the *Univers*, taken from *Figaro*, in which it was said that among the Zouaves who had been killed was one distinguished for his bravery, Giulio Watts-Russell, aged twenty-one. The name was that of his younger, the age that of his elder son; it might therefore be either the one or the other, perhaps both.

He made the sacrifice in his heart.

He came quickly to Rome, where, during his short stay, it was no small consolation to him to hear, from so many quarters, especially from Wilfrid, all the circumstances of the last days, the death and funeral, of his dearest Giulio.

His recent journey in Spain was itself a consolation to him from its pleasing recollections. On referring to dates, he found that a few days before the battle of Mentana, he had remained to pray for his two beloved sons in the place where S. Ignatius had received his memorable wound at the siege of Pampeluna. Besides which, on the very morning of the 3rd of November, he and his daughter had received Holy Communion in the celebrated Sanctuary of *Our Lady of the Pillar*,—the first place in the world consecrated by a miraculous apparition of the Mother of God, and there he had prayed especially for Wilfrid and Giulio, and had recommended them to Mary; and besides this he had been accustomed to practise in his family, at three o'clock in the afternoon, a short devotion in honour of the Agony of Jesus, recommending those in their agony to His Divine mercy, with these words, *"Miserere animæ agonizantis in egressu suo;"* and thus, on the 3rd of November, at three o'clock, without knowing it, he had recommended the soul of his son, who precisely at that hour (allowing for the difference of meridian) died on the field of Mentana.

From the many edifying things which he heard at Rome of Giulio, by overcoming through the abundance of grace the feelings of nature, he was constrained more than once to repeat those first words of his—"I am satisfied." He expressed his gratitude for the honours which had been paid to the body in carrying it from Mentana to Rome, adding, however, that if he had been on the spot, he would not have thought of taking his Giulio from the noble obscurity of a burial in Mentana, which was before God the true field of his glory. Neither did he wish to accept the affectionate proposal of transporting the body to England, for he felt that if he must select a place, he could not choose a better than the cemetery of Rome, near the tombs of the Martyrs.

A beautiful marble cross, and at its foot, a laurel crown, with the monogram of Christ in the centre, and an inscription engraved on the pedestal, mark his tomb. Such is the simple monument of this young soldier of Christ! In the inscription occurs his true baptismal name, "Julianus," although he was commonly called Giulio, not only in Italy, but even in England, and especially in his family, who used it as an endearing abbreviation for Julian. The marble cross is situated in the first row upon the slope of the rising ground, near the monument of an English officer, General Tylee, of the Indian army, who, having come to Rome with his wife for the Easter of 1865, died a holy death in my arms, within a month of his arrival, returning thanks to God, Who had brought him to die in the holy city, and because his body would rest near the tombs of the Martyrs. I had learnt at the death-bed of the General a devout act of praise repeated by him almost at his last moments, in honour of the Most August Trinity; and what was my surprise when I discovered it in Giulio's little book of devotions, who, without having the least acquaintance with the General, learnt this prayer from a simple account in a letter that I wrote to his father. Who would have thought that within so short a time, it would have been my lot to lay this young hero side by side with that brave General?

But I have not mentioned something else in that little book of Giulio's, which is well worthy of note—I mean a long act of devotion to the most Holy Virgin, which I hear he recited daily, although he had promised to repeat it only every Saturday. In it he specially begs to be free from temptations at the point of death, and expresses his desire to carry this protest always with him, even to the last moment of his life, as a pledge of his devotion to Mary, and as a challenge to all the powers of hell; he even desired it should be buried with him. It is evident, since his death was instantaneous, that the devil had no time to tempt him. Moreover, he took this little book with him on his march to the battlefield, as his companion. The only thing which remained was, that it should be buried with him; and, without knowing it, I had an opportunity granted me even to do this. For the consolation of the father, who heard so much of the remarkable suppleness of his son's body, I obtained leave for its disinterment without his making any request for it; it was then that Giulio's sister copied from the little book that protest, and the father with his own hand placed it upon the breast of his devoted son.

This happened on Saturday, the 23rd of November, twenty

days after his death, and was certainly no small consolation to the father, the sister, and the brother, and the few friends who accompanied them, to see the body once more, and to conduct it back to the Cemetery Church, where the Holy Mass was celebrated, and all communicated. The day afterwards they all left Rome, gladdened with what they had seen: for as Mr. Watts-Russell expressed it, no description could have made him comprehend the extraordinary flexibility of the body, which seemed to have robbed death of one of its most terrible trophies. Wilfrid was also obliged to leave Rome with his father, hoping that with the change of climate the fever would abate, and that he might recover his strength. Shortly after they left Rome the two military decorations which had been so well deserved by him and his brother, were forwarded to him.

This military cross, commemorating the campaign of 1867, and which decorates the breasts of so many pontifical soldiers, is much the same as the celebrated cross of Castelfidardo, on which was inscribed the motto, *"Pro Sede Petri."* The new decoration is of silver, and in the form of a Maltese Cross, having in its centre a medallion, which bears on one side a cross with the motto, *"Hinc Victoria,"* and on the other the tiara and keys, with the motto, *"Fide et Virtuti,"* and at the outer edge, Pius P.P. IX. an. MDCCCLXVII. But that which most honours the brave men who consecrated their life and blood to so holy a cause, is the first sentence of the pontifical brief, in which, after having instituted the commemorative decoration, Pius IX. inscribes the following eulogy:—"That they have indeed deserved well of the Pontiff, the Apostolic See, and the Catholic cause."

CHAPTER III.

Some account of Giulio's life: the happy omen in his Baptismal name.

THE glory of Giulio is his death. As then I have begun this memoir with this proposition, so I could close it by applying to him the words of Martial—

"Scire piget post tale decus quid fecerit ante."

On the other hand, a glorious death reflects its lustre, and throws I know not what enchantment on all the "little events," even the most minute, of the whole life, verifying in this way the saying of Petrarch—

"Un bel morir tutta la vita onora."

It becomes, then, a pleasant task now to review and retrace the short life of Giulio, and so, little by little, to bring the truth of these words home to ourselves by observing how nature and grace worked together throughout his whole life, and prepared him for so beautiful a death. It is precisely in this that my new memoir differs from that which I wrote before in the *Divin Salvatore*, which was simply an account of his death, with the addition of a few particulars of his life; for this has increased so much as to become a little biography. It is true that I feel some restraint in writing, from the modesty of Giulio's nearest relations, and especially of his father, who shrinks from publicity, and is afraid that I have made too much of him, even in my first memoir.

But though I respect his modesty, I can now speak with greater liberty, especially since Mr. Watts-Russell, condescending to my desire, answered me in these words, "All that you think well to do I acquiesce in, *ex animo*. I regard Giulio as belonging to God, and to me only in a very secondary manner; and if it is thought better to publish a more ample account of the grace he has received, I do not think that I have any right to say nay."

To begin then from the beginning, the very name which was given him in Baptism, in a way which was somewhat remarkable, brought with it a happy omen for the future. He was born on the Epiphany of 1850, in Florence, where at that time the family were residing; and the father communicated this new joy by letter to a holy Nun, to whose prayers he and the mother had recommended this birth. The Nun sent a reply on the 11th Jany., and although she probably supposed that the infant had been already baptized, she nevertheless suggested three names, *Gaspar*, *Michael*, and *Julian*, saying: "Of these three names select that which you like best, provided only he be placed under the holy protection of all, for they perchance one day will obtain for him from Heaven the necessary qualities to combat victoriously the enemies of our holy religion (*"qui lui obtiendra peutetre un jour du ciel les qualites necessaires pour combattre victorieusement les ennemis de notre sainte religion"*). These words have now received a definite and precise sense which could not then naturally have been imagined. Had the Baptism taken place at the time originally determined on, this letter would have been too late; but nevertheless it happened to be in time, on account of this holy Sacrament having been deferred for several days in order that H. E. Card. Piccolomini, who had made a promise, and even a courteous request to baptize the infant, might conveniently attend.

The Cardinal was then residing at his villa near Sienna, but through the loss of the first letter, and a heavy fall of snow which happened at that time, he was unable to come.

The Archbishop and the Nuncio courteously offered to fill the Cardinal's place; but Mr. Watts-Russell, who had waited for some days—not with any view to the prestige of the Baptism, but only because of his promise—modestly refused these honourable offers, and without waiting any longer, on the 15th January, brought the child to the sacred Font. But the letter of the holy Nun already referred to arrived in good time, just as he was going out of his house. When he read it, it seemed to him to have been providential that he had deferred the holy ceremony for so long a time; especially it appeared strange that the Religious should have supposed that it was possible to change the names which had been already fixed by Baptism. In short, they gladly accepted these three names, and moreover added to them the name of *Mary*. And so the infant received for his first name, *Julian*, which, afterwards, as I have said, was shortened by his family into the endearing name of *Giulio*.

In another letter, written on the 22nd of February, 1850, the holy Nun added an allusion to the martyr, S. Julian, whose feast is celebrated on the 9th of January, in the following words: "S. Julian, the Martyr of Antioch, combined a simple wisdom with purity and courage—virtues so much to be longed for in these sad days, and which I ardently desire for my little Julian, ... so it will not be wonderful if God, in His own time, grants him the grace, as He did to S. Julian, to follow in practices of virtue that innumerable company of noble souls who, like him, did not fear to give their lives for the defence of our holy religion." Here is truly a happy Christian omen in Julian's birth, which has so beautiful an echo in his death.

Certainly from different accounts which I have received, and from many things which I shall mention in this memoir, it seems that the good odour of his youthful sacrifice, which he diffused wherever he was known, drew oftentimes many souls to God, more perchance than his example in a far longer life could have done.

These most happy omens were confirmed a few months later by the same Religious, in a conversation with Giulio's mother, to whom she spoke as if not she, but Mary herself with her own mouth, had given these names to her beloved child, assuring her that Mary would be always a mother to him. The way in which *she* said this impressed her with an idea that she would not live long to be a mother to him, although she was at that time in perfect health: and this presentiment was indeed fully verified.

CHAPTER IV.

The Mother of Giulio.

AS I have mentioned Giulio's Mother, I cannot finish my little memoir without leaving a flower on her tomb, and thus interweaving the name of the pious Augusta Maria Watts-Russell with that of Giulio. It will not be a vain conjecture if we attribute her having been blessed with so noble a son to the piety of her life, and the many prayers which she offered previous to his birth.

Feeling great anxiety because of the extreme danger attending her last confinement, she gave herself more than ever to prayer. Besides other devotions, by the advice of a saintly Religious (Sister Mary Louisa of Jesus, of the third order of Servites at Naples) she recited nine *"Hail Marys"* for several months, recommending the birth to Mary Immaculate. On the eve of her confinement, with a holy simplicity, she swallowed a little wafer on which a Religious of the Servites of Mary had written, *"Blessed be the Holy and Immaculate Conception of the Blessed Virgin Mary."* Almost immediately after swallowing this, she was happily delivered of a boy without any danger, although on other similar occasions she had suffered so much. She even felt herself in a better state of health than ever for a whole year, up to the 30th of January, 1851, which may be said to be the last day of her health. Even on that day, the very last thing which she did was an act of special devotion for Giulio; for being at that time in Rome, she wished to fulfil her long-cherished desire of performing the devotion of *Scala Santa* with her husband and all her little children, consisting of two girls and two boys, and Giulio, just thirteen months old, whom she carried in her arms as she ascended the *Holy Stairs* on her knees. She had been in the morning to the House of S. Frances of Rome, in the *Trastevere*, where the Holy Father said Mass, in order that she might have the consolation of receiving Communion from his hands. In that house at that time there was a department for pious exercises, and fifty-nine poor children were gathered there in order to prepare for their first Communion, which the Holy Father, Pius IX., on that morning gave to them with his own hand, having first addressed them with such fervour that he drew tears from the eyes not only of the children, but also of the ladies and gentlemen who had come there to receive the Body of Christ from the hands of His Vicar. It was a bright and happy day for Mrs. Watts-Russell. But the weather was cold, and she was obliged to kneel in a draught. This was the beginning of her slow but fatal illness. It may indeed be said that when the devout lady on that very afternoon (with Giulio in her arms and her other children around her) ascended the holy stairs upon her knees with great devotion, she truly began her own *"via crucis!"* An attack of consumption, patiently endured for nine months, brought her to the completion of her sacrifice, at Venice, on the 11th of November, 1851, by a death so holy that, to use the expression of two Priests who assisted at it (Don Luigi Tonini and Don Jacopo Vitturi), "She seemed to them to see an angel who was eagerly waiting to conduct her into the presence of God."

At the hour of her death she fervently recommended all her children to God and to the protection of the Blessed Virgin; and an Image of Mary which her husband held before her, almost to her last moments, was one of her sweetest consolations in her agony.

Her death was an echo of her life, all love towards God, her family, and the poor. Everybody loved her, for there was a grace in her words and a charm in her manners which went straight to all hearts, especially to the hearts of the poor. When she was living at the Baths of Lucca, she used every Thursday to have four of the oldest poor men of the place, selected by the curate, to dine at her house. She used always to serve them at table, not allowing the servants to do anything, assisted only by her two little girls. And this she did with such an absence of all false shame, that what in another might have seemed strange and unnatural, appeared in her to flow without effort from a heart that was kindled by Divine Grace.

These same qualities appeared very beautifully upon another occasion, when she had dressed herself with more than ordinary care to go and make some visits in Florence.

In passing through the street, she saw a poor rag-gatherer fall down at a door-step in a fainting fit. He was exceedingly dirty and repulsive in appearance, and the place very public; but without a moment's hesitation she went to the man's assistance. She sent her husband into the nearest house for a glass of water and bathed his face and temples with her handkerchief, and did not leave the poor man until he had recovered. I may also mention of her that she had stripped herself of all her jewels and ornaments with very few exceptions for purposes of charity or as offerings to God. The last she retained was a bracelet, which had a particular value from having been given her by the Dowager-Queen of Bavaria, but this also she at last presented to the shrine of S. Mary Magdalen of Pazzi, at Florence.

After such proofs of her virtues as these, we cannot wonder that Father Germinano, who was her confessor in Rome, wished that her husband should write her life: but his feelings were far too keen for such an attempt; and besides, her history was so interwoven with his own, that his modesty would never have permitted him to desire, for his wife, this well-deserved eulogy.

But I wish to pay liberally this little tribute to Giulio's mother; and to add, that her living praise and glory are in very truth her children. The two daughters, Augusta and Ellen, heirs of their mother's piety, would both have been Religious had health been granted them: of three sons John is already a Passionist, while Wilfrid and Giulio have distinguished themselves as soldiers of the Cross.

CHAPTER V.

The First Years of Giulio, in his Family.

THOUGH Giulio had not the happiness of knowing his mother, he was not therefore deprived of the good and pious education which he would have received from her. The bright years of an innocent childhood were passed under the shadow of his family in England, Italy, and France. He was a particularly gentle boy, full of good and affectionate feelings; and his beauty of person, his intelligence, and winning manners attracted everybody.

Father Faber's name is so dear and venerable that it is not wonderful if I should reckon it to have been one of Giulio's greatest graces that he should have had him for his confessor when quite a little boy. That great mind knew so well how to captivate children, that (like S. Philip, who had a speciality for the young) he cast into the innocent soul the first seeds of the love of Jesus and Mary, when he heard the little penitent's first confession. Moreover, on account of his long-standing friendship with Mr. Watts-Russell, he had a particular affection for the three little children, who therefore in the first years, during which they lived in London, near the Oratory, were, so to say, under the shadow of S. Philip. They used often to go to the Oratory, and Father Faber frequently asked the boys to come and stay with him at the country house of the Oratorians at Sydenham, where they enjoyed innocent amusements; as some of these good fathers affectionately remember. In 1857 Giulio, then not more than seven years old, came to Rome, and remained for two months, together with his two brothers, in the *"Collegio Nobili"* under the Jesuit Fathers: but soon the whole family returned to Venice, and there Giulio and his brother John received the Holy Sacrament of Confirmation on the third Sunday in September, 1857. Of that day, long to be remembered by a soldier of Christ, the Priest Don Joseph Calderan, their master, who was on that occasion their Godfather, wrote to me as follows:—

"That day, I assure you, was for me one of the brightest in my life. What preparation! What thoughtfulness! What fervent prayer! I really imagined myself to be between two angels at that function which the Patriarch Ramazotti performed at the Church of the Pianto."

The same Priest told me a little incident, which showed me how Giulio, when only a child, possessed a heart open to charity.

"One day I went, according to my custom, to the Convent of the Discalced Carmelites, and saw one of the fathers who was ill (Father Octavius of S. John Baptist); and, happening to be present when he took a restorative, the little boy, without any one suggesting it to him, returned to the house and begged his father to be allowed to take back something better for the sick man; but he was told that Religious were accustomed to abstain from flesh meat, and could never taste any of the good things which even the sick poor were able to eat. So he and his two brothers brought back some *magro* food to the cell, saying to him, 'Father Octavius, we have asked Papa to give us some meat for you, which would have done you good.' And so they continued for some days carrying from their own dinners to the Convent everything which Father Octavius was able to eat; and he accepted with grateful pleasure, not so much the food, as the charity of these young hearts."

From Venice in the autumn of 1858, Mr. Watts-Russell went with his family to Rome, and wishing to provide his sons with an excellent tutor, invited to his house a gentleman, who for three years educated them in letters and piety, until they entered the College of Ushaw, in England. At my request he has given me a slight sketch of the character of his young pupil, and he has done it so beautifully that it appears to me to be a photograph of him, in which the light comes out more clearly from its contrast with the shadows. He writes—

"One of the most beautiful traits in the character of Giulio Watts-Russell was the rapidity with which, when he had committed any fault, he rushed at reparation. I have seen him, after a moment's irritation, plunged in such quick sorrow that he seemed to have scarcely time to change rebellion for repentance. The natural swiftness of his mind and heart would make him see an error before he had wrought it to completion; and the goodness which he had by grace and education rendered him much more edifying in his weakness than most people in their virtue and constraint. I am writing with the remembrance of the time when I had the privilege to be his tutor: and I often thought, when contemplating both his merits and defects. Of such material must be those who are destined to be saints. Without the least attempt at panegyric, I should boldly say that from nine years old to seventeen Giulio was a type of Catholic youth."

Some months before going to college, Giulio having reached his eleventh year, made his first Communion at Rochecorbon near Tours; but I have nothing special to say of this great day of his life, with which I close this first period of an innocent and devout childhood spent among his family.

CHAPTER VI.

The Years spent by Giulio in College.

GIULIO was at Ushaw from the middle of 1861 almost to January, 1863. There is little in the routine of a college life that would possess any interest. But it is worthy of remark that, just as his private tutor in his own home, so also at college, those who were immediately over him, observed, as a beautiful characteristic trait in Giulio, his promptitude in discovering and correcting his faults: that good practice which I mentioned at the beginning of the memoir continued almost to the last, for when, not long before his death, he was impatient with his dear brother, he at once uttered those sweet words, "Wilfrid, let us kneel down and make an act of contrition, and then shake hands."

I am told that at college he received correction in such good dispositions and with such an open acknowledgment of his having deserved it, that it was impossible to feel angry with him. His natural temperament was so lively, and he was so fond of amusement and bold adventures, that he not unfrequently got into scrapes; and in a college so well disciplined as Ushaw such faults could not pass unnoticed. I do not wish to deceive, I am not writing a panegyric, or even the life of a saint. Nay, it appears to me that Giulio smiles on me from heaven (if I may speak so boldly) more for writing about his defects, than for recording his virtues. The defect was momentary, and the penitence followed almost immediately, but it did not cease so quickly, and indeed to his good companions at college, who knew him so well, I should wish to say: "If any of you marked in him any defect, I am certain that Giulio amply lamented it."

There was one little fault in his childhood more worthy of laughter than of blame, about which I shall not be silent, for it reveals his independent and generous character.

A short time after he came to college he wrote a romantic naval adventure, entitled, "Ran to the Sea," in which he describes himself as a hero who sailed to Australia in a little boat. The process of writing the tale so worked upon his young and ardent imagination, that, although he was very happy at college, he resolved to brave romantic perils and adventures.

Without saying anything to his brothers, he set off, with another little boy still younger than himself, to the nearest seaport, about twelve miles off, in order to get on board a vessel and find some strange adventure. The little knights errant had only about two shillings between them for their expenses, and they turned their coats inside out by way of disguise. Of course when the boys were missed, search was made, and many went in pursuit of the fugitives.

They were overtaken about four miles from the college, about nightfall, having lost their way, very tired and hungry, and, I dare say, glad to be caught. Giulio received a reprimand for a fault which the college could not, of course, pass over; but the simplicity and penitence of the poor child under this little trial were very touching. The whole adventure ended in a little punishment: but it was oftentimes the cause of great amusement among his companions; and when at last the news of his glorious death reached Ushaw, some of them said, "Giulio ran away from Ushaw, but he did not fly before the muskets at Mentana." His father, in a letter of correction which he wrote to his son on the occasion of his running away, told him that if he so much loved adventure and romance, he must leave the Blessed Virgin to direct his life for him, instead of doing it for himself, and then perhaps she would weave it into a more romantic tale than he could possibly picture to himself. Mr. Watts-Russell observed that these words kept a place in his son's memory, and when he was speaking (as we said before) of going either to Austria or Rome, and when the projects pleased him simply because he felt attracted by them, he was somewhat afraid of again forestalling the Providence of God, and engaging in a new career which might not be designed for him; and so that anecdote of his life at college seems to have cast an influence over him to the end; and this is another strong reason for not passing it over in silence.

The life at college gave him likewise an opportunity of showing certain traits in his social character which would not so easily have unfolded themselves in the restricted circles of his family. His great openness and candour, his kind manners to all around him, his respectful deference, united with an affectionate familiarity towards his superiors, made him much beloved by all who had the charge of him; and as for his companions, I am told that there was hardly a boy who was a greater favourite with his equals; for he was exceedingly generous, kind, and good-tempered. Indeed, when the time for his leaving the college arrived, many of his companions shed tears on parting with him; and he retained to the last an affectionate remembrance of many whom he left behind him.

But what is far more important to record is that during the last year which he spent at college, a great spiritual change for the better seemed to come over him. He was always good, but among so many good boys there was nothing remarkable in him; and I believe that he was more esteemed for what they *knew* lay beneath the surface than for what appeared; since many treasures of grace lay hidden under the natural virtues of his character which attracted the eyes of men. But as he grew older, at the age of thirteen or fourteen, he appeared to derive great profit, even externally, from his college education, and the work of grace on so good a foundation was clearly manifested. He became more and more devout; and though as full as ever of fun and good humour, he was most attentive to his prayers and all his religious duties. With such a temperament as his it is manifest that this would require far more effort than in ordinary cases. It is no wonder, therefore, that one of the prefects who had immediate charge of him, from what he saw during the last year, felt a strong conviction that God would give him in the end a vocation to the priesthood, and that Giulio would be one of those who have gone forth from that flourishing seminary to work in God's vineyard in England.

But the Lord, in the mysterious order of his graces, had reserved for Giulio another vocation, and if Ushaw cannot reckon this *"alumnus"* among her apostolic missionaries, she can, however, in very truth, number him amongst her glories.

CHAPTER VII.

The Last Years of Giulio in his Family.

IT was Mr. Watts-Russell's intention to keep his sons for some years in Rome, where they might be able to complete their studies; but their health would not permit of this protracted stay; and so the last years of Giulio's life were spent partly in Italy and partly in France, Corsica, Germany, and England. In January, 1863, the three brothers came from Ushaw to Rome, and it was then that I, as the spiritual director and friend of the father, had the pleasure of knowing these good youths, although I was not their confessor. They followed their studies with profit under the direction of Don Liberato, whom I myself presented to Mr. Watts-Russell as master and chaplain of the family. It is not necessary to say more of the character of Giulio than that as he increased in years he grew stronger in manly virtues, such as a holy contempt for anything mean and base, and a love for everything noble and self-sacrificing. He was always ready to oblige others, whatever trouble it might cost him: he was also fearless of danger, especially when it was a question of doing good to others, as he proved in the summer of 1865, when, being 15 years old, he threw himself into the river Loire, to save from drowning a little peasant boy named Dupuis, whom he was rejoiced to restore safe and sound to his family. The little boy had fallen into the Loire, where he would have been infallibly drowned in the deep and rapid stream, had not Giulio plunged in to save him, at considerable risk to his own life; for at that time he had only just learnt how to swim.

To this generous soul he joined a most affectionate disposition, and especially towards his father, whom he treated with the tenderness of a daughter; and I have heard that at Vouvray, whilst the father was lying in bed with a severe nervous illness, Giulio, sitting down beside him and not able to give him any ease, burst into tears more than once.

On the whole, the life at Vouvray was a very happy one, being divided between works of piety, study, and domestic amusements: from thence the father wrote to me, saying, "my boys go on very regularly, piously, and happily, indeed we are always a very gay and cheerful party;" and my friend Don Liberato wrote to me to thank me, and said that he seemed to be living not with a family of Seculars, but in the house of Religious; and to speak only of Giulio—for he wrote to me especially about him—he told me that the youth took the greatest interest in the very beautiful pastoral letters of the French Bishops; and that, with a wisdom far above his years, he often talked with his master of the doctrines of the Church, and of the prominent errors of the day, in order to bring his own views into exact conformity with the teaching of Holy Church.

He told me also that, when he went out for any recreation, it gave him very great pleasure to hear some account of the lives of the Saints; and especially he often mentioned his wish to assist as far as he could in the Apostolic ministry of missionaries, when they should be settled in Australia, a project which had been often mooted during the whole of that year, but which was destined never to be accomplished.

It may perchance seem to be an intrusion to speak of a family project which was never carried into effect, but I hope that I may be pardoned if I lift the veil a little from the private life of a family, by relating some things which had so great an interest in the heart and life of Giulio, at Vouvray; since not only actions, but also thoughts and desires make up our lives, especially before God.

Already for a long time Mr. Watts-Russell had been reflecting, that it is the most difficult part of education to find some employment in life which is suitable to young men, who had at such an early age finished their education at college; for then the question arises, what are they to do? For doing nothing is the worst profession of all. The army, the navy, the law possess indeed advantages, but they are full of dangers, especially to young Catholics in England.

He thought that if he and all his family, with a Priest as Chaplain, could have gone, as several English gentlemen had done, into some English Colony, and there bought a farm, and invested their capital in it, the young men would have an innocent and active career open to them without much danger: they would live together, their religious and intellectual life would not be neglected, and they would enjoy all the advantages of home, and at the same time the country pursuits so dear to Englishmen.

Mr. Watts-Russell fully perceived that the project had its dark side; that it had dangers and risks, and grave difficulties to be overcome. But finally, after much thought, counsel, and prayer, he laid his project before his sons as a family design. They continued to think of it from the beginning; and indeed through the whole year which they spent at Vouvray. Australia was the common topic of the thoughts, conversation, and devotions of the family.

Don Liberato, who was to have gone with them, told me that he often heard the young men singing together a short hymn to *Our Lady, Star of the Sea*, asking her aid to obtain a prosperous voyage to Australia. They hoped that their home and Chaplain would have become a little centre for Catholics, where many might unite, who otherwise would be cut off from the Sacraments of the Church. The future Missionary intended proposing to the Bishop of Brisbane to place this new Missionary establishment under the Invocation of S. Francis Xavier; and Miss Watts-Russell had a scheme of her own to carry out a small number of English Carmelite Nuns. But above all, the three brothers, for whom this project was especially formed, used to picture in gay colours to themselves the career which they imagined to lie before them in Australia. Giulio recollected with pleasure his own little book "Ran to the Sea," and what he called his *Daring Flight*, which was the most exciting incident in his childhood. It was all castle-building. But does not a great portion of our life consist in castle-building, and the remaining portion in the architecture of our castles? for (to use a beautiful expression of Father Faber's) it is a great point to know what is the spirit which animates us, and what the spiritual age which we have reached. Certainly, to speak only of Giulio, I believe that he possesses a reward in Heaven for his beautiful castle in the air, of doing the work of a Catechist to assist the Australian Missionary; but he has a far more glorious crown for his resignation in seeing his castle fall into ruins; since failures, disappointments, and thwarted desires are often, more than successes, the first gems in our heavenly crowns.

The project was disapproved of by some friends: legal difficulties were made, especially with regard to the transfer of the funds; and when the first trials were overcome others arose. The scheme appeared indeed at one time on the point of being carried out, but it eventually came to nothing: however as their long cherished Australian scheme hung always suspended on the will of God, they were ready to give up their own wishes, and to accept the change from God's blessed Providence, with a feeling, not only of submission, but of thankfulness and love. And so in that trial in which it must have been very hard to young hearts to see their golden dreams vanish, they often comforted themselves by repeating that cheerful saying of S. Philip Neri—

"Vi ringrazio mio Dio

Perche non van le cose a modo mio."[3]

Graceful lines! which I had taught them when they were at Rome, and which they repeated with great pleasure on this occasion. When this scheme was given up, the future Missionary returned to his parish in Italy; and, a little while after Mr. Watts-Russell, instead of passing another winter at Vouvray, the climate of which he had found too severe, went with his family to try the mild air of Ajaccio. The residence in Ajaccio was a beautiful period in the spiritual life of Giulio, for just as in the last year at Ushaw, so now in the first months in Ajaccio, they saw clearly a new shower of grace descending on him to perfect his character. He was much impressed by the sermons of a Franciscan monk, who went to preach during Advent, 1865. To him Giulio made a general confession, and from that time forward, though he was always good, he became happier and better than ever; whilst at the same time he was more deeply impressed with the fear of God. There was added to the natural gaiety of his character, a seriousness of purpose which he did not before possess, and he used to listen to all religious instructions and conversations with an earnestness which delighted his Father.

He began at that time to practise little mortifications, which would escape the notice of all who did not know him well: then, for the first time in his life, he fasted in order to gain the jubilee. His devotion to the poor was also quite

---

[3] I give thanks to Thee, my God, because things do not happen as I wish.

remarkable, and he seemed to grow daily and rapidly in piety and virtue; so much so that it was a constant subject of conversation between his father and his eldest sister. It was then also that he adopted that beautiful maxim—

"Anima mia, anima mia,

Ama Dio e tira via."

I could add other praises of Giulio from a letter which I have received from the Canon Luigi Forcioli, who knew him intimately in Ajaccio; but since he is so eloquent, and panegyrises, not only Giulio, but also the whole family, I will not quote from it, or other similar letters which I have received from various places, for they are hardly in conformity with the simplicity of this memoir.

While he was in Ajaccio, a new scheme was discussed for his future career, but like the other, it was destined to come to nothing.

When the German war broke out, a General in the Austrian service, who was a near connection of theirs, offered to obtain commissions in the Austrian army for Wilfrid and Giulio, the latter being just sixteen years old: their brother John, who came between them in age, had already resolved to take up the cross rather than the sword, and to offer himself as a Passionist in England. Wilfrid and Giulio wished to accept the offer, and to buckle on their swords, not so much for the Kaiser as for the cause of religion and order, which they considered him to represent; and their father sent them off in God's Name. Obstacles however presented themselves. It was necessary that they should obtain the Queen's permission before entering a foreign service; and this could not be given without a breach of neutrality. So the English government prevented their entering the Austrian service, a prohibition, however, which opened the way to a service far more glorious. Thus their first military project was nipped in the bud; still on that occasion they went through a good deal of drilling; and so, what they underwent in order to become officers in the Austrian army helped them to become simple privates among the crusaders of the Pope.

Thus they passed the summer of 1866 at Gräz and at Munich, in the house of a near relation. Somebody who at that time closely observed Giulio wrote to me these simple words about him, which unite together his gifts of grace and nature. "I found in him certainly a piety far above his sixteen years, but the gaiety of his heart and the impetuosity of his fresh young life answered to his tender age."

From Germany they returned to England, to Ilam Hall, the residence of their grandfather, whither Mr. Watts-Russell already had gone with his daughter and also his second son, who wished to become a Religious, an object which he accomplished a short while after the return of his brothers from Germany.

However, on the evening before the separation, the farewell parting was nearly being changed into great mourning. Whilst the good novice was preparing devoutly for his parting, his two brothers playfully took down two old muskets, which had been for years hanging in the hall, in order that they might lay wait for him in the passage and pretend to shoot him. They put caps on the guns to make a noise; but one of them happening to be loaded, the ball passed so near his head, as he turned the corner of the passage, that his escape was really wonderful. They all went down on their knees immediately to thank God for so great a deliverance. It was on the feast of S. Michael, 29th of September, 1866, that John left the world, being then about eighteen and a half years old. His name in Religion is now Brother Michael of the Sacred Heart of Mary: he made his vows on the Feast of the Divine Maternity, 16th of October, 1867; and thus was offering his peaceful sacrifice at the very time in which his brothers were preparing to give their lives in defence of the See of Peter. And here I will add that when I received the letter which contained the news of John's entering the noviciate of the Passionists, at Broadway, I said to myself "now we shall see that Giulio will have a vocation to the company of Jesus" (for he would have made an excellent Jesuit): but it was not I who said this of Giulio first, but another who knew him far better than I.

Meanwhile Wilfrid and Giulio spent a very pleasant life at the family residence of Ilam Hall, for some months, earning always more and more the affection of their grandfather and Mrs. Watts-Russell; until in the spring of 1867, they started for Rome, among several other English Catholics who had the grace and the glory to fight for the See of Peter.

CHAPTER VIII.

Giulio becomes a Zouave.

DIRECTLY the two generous brothers perceived that a storm was about to burst forth against Rome, they determined to become Zouaves, and their father wrote to me about it on the 18th of April, 1867; but in the answer which I sent back, I rather threw cold water on their fervour on purpose to try them. Nevertheless they came at once to Rome, and very soon after their arrival in the Holy City they called upon me, and then I received them most warmly, and immediately took them to the Chapels of S. Aloysius and Blessed John Berchmans, where the young Zouaves, and especially the Belgians and Dutch, went often to pray. They soon after enlisted, and were presented to me in the Zouave uniform by the Count de Redmond, who died (before Giulio) of the cholera, a victim to his charity. They immediately inured themselves to the noble daily sacrifice of the laborious and humble life of private soldiers: and Giulio told me laughing, that he soon learnt how to clean the leggings.

One month after their arrival, they, with all the other

Zouaves, were filled with new fervour on witnessing that grand solemnity of the Centenary of S. Peter. It may be said with truth that, on this great occasion, the Zouaves were not only spectators of this pageant, but also "a spectacle" to the whole Catholic world: and, after the sight of the Bishops, whose presence in such numbers round the Chair of S. Peter, made more than ever manifest the unity of the Church, nothing attracted the eyes and the admiration of foreigners so much as this large body of Catholic youths, gathered together to defend the Holy See with their blood.

Among the many compositions in different languages which were published during those days was one in Portuguese entitled *"A exposicao universal de Roma em 1867,"*[4] in which, contrasting the Universal Exposition in Paris with the spectacle in Rome, it remarked with reason that among so many marvels of virtue and moral progress, and true Catholic greatness which Rome manifested before the world, these soldiers of the Pope, reproducing the ancient Crusaders, were pre-eminent. I myself saw not a few of them praying fervently at the Altar, where at that time was exposed the true chair of S. Peter, guarded day and night by Priests and soldiers; and I saw them (by the hand of the Priests) touch this sacred Relic with their beads and their bayonets, and then kneel down, and offer up to God with new fervour the hidden sacrifices of their military life in barracks, as well as the more glorious sacrifices of the battle field. In this army, which for very many of them might truly be called a

---

4   Roma expora ao mundo os antigos Cruzados reproduzidos nos militares Pontificaes. (Omaggio Cattolico, p. 350)

religious military order, the short life of Giulio was like a fervent noviciate. In their barrack room, upon first waking in the morning, he and his brother continued to the last their old habit of greeting each other with the words "Praised be Jesus and Mary," to which the other answered "now and for ever:" and to so good a beginning responded the whole day, which they ended by reciting together the evening prayers.

I have conversed with several Zouaves who were Giulio's companions, and they have all spoken of him to me with a singular feeling of esteem and affection.

One young Zouave who was his intimate friend, in a letter to his father, which, though it was not intended for publication, was inserted in the *Westminster Gazette*, spoke of Giulio's death in the following affectionate terms. "There was one terrible drawback to the battle, however, and that was the death of the youngest of the Watts-Russells; I cannot tell you how I felt it; he was one of the best fellows I ever met, but if any one has gone to Heaven he has, for he was half a saint." The writer of this letter became a Zouave some time before Giulio; and I am glad to say that he was the first soldier friend to whom I introduced the two brothers. On this account I asked him to write to me something about Giulio, as he wrote to his father from Monte Rotondo. He has therefore favoured me with the following: "As long as I knew Giulio, which was more than four months, I never heard from him anything approaching to a bad or irreverent word. Whenever by any chance anyone said anything bad before him, he would immediately ask him to stop, and if he did not, he would walk away. Nearly always when we were out walking and passed a Church he would ask us to go in and pray for a few minutes. Always, whilst he was at the depôt with me, he would say his Rosary every evening, however tired he was, and whatever hard work he had been doing all day. Every morning that he possibly could, he used to go to Mass, and stay in the Church some length of time afterwards. He used to go to confession very often and very regularly; and whatever he had to do, however pleasant and agreeable, he would not put that off. A serjeant told me that he used to go every day between the drill hours to a little chapel, close to the depôt; and that one day, happening to pass that way, he saw him kneeling so devoutly at the foot of the large Cross there, that he also went up; and both kissed the foot of the Crucifix. Every one who knew him has the same opinion of him, and says that he never met even those he disliked with crossness, but shook hands with everyone, and treated all in the same kind and pleasing manner."

These simple words, which say so much, appear to me to be like a beautiful panegyric, and I am glad that Serjeant Woodward was not in Rome, for I would far rather have received these words in writing than *vivâ voce*. Another friend of Giulio's, an Irish serjeant, has spoken to me several times of him, with the tenderness and vehemence of an Irish heart, and so also have two English friends of his, who held the rank of corporals. Another Irish friend who was near him at Mentana, said to me, with an ingenuous feeling of holy envy, "he deserved to die, he was so good." Another

Zouave told me that he never grumbled, that he always gave way to his brother, and in order to show even more strongly the extent of his deference to his brother, he added, "he was very obedient to him."

They also remarked in Giulio a promptness to oblige others, even to his own personal inconvenience.

And then, if sometimes he was ordered to do duty for another, he did not ask "why;" but he took the place assigned to him at once and with good humour. Others indeed have told me that they have observed nothing particular in him excepting that he was very good; and although there was nothing remarkable about him, he rejoiced in the esteem of most and the affection of all; which I think is great praise.

To the testimonies which the Zouaves have given agree those of others, and especially of the Chevalier Geneste, who, during the time which he spent in Rome, knew him more intimately every day. He, almost as soon as the two brothers had arrived in Rome, offered them his house as their home. He knew Giulio from a child of seven years old; and he performed the last offices for his dead body.

The day before they enlisted as Zouaves, Giulio came to his house full of joy, and said to him, "Signor Geneste, I have some news for you which will please you very much: I feel sure that you will never guess it;" but Signor Geneste guessed it immediately, and lamented that he had not told them to join directly they arrived in Rome; and Giulio said, "I did not wish to tell you till to-day, because we wanted to give you a surprise by appearing before you in the Zouave uniform; but now it is accomplished." Signor Geneste then gave his hand to the two brothers, and congratulated them warmly on their happiness.

The Countess de Redmond told me that in her familiar intercourse with Giulio during these last months, it was a source of devotion to her to see this young man at the same time so joyful and thoughtful; and that open joy which shone in his face seemed to her to be due not so much to the freshness of his youth as to the innocence of his heart, to such an extent that though she knew him so well, yet she felt reverence as well as affection for him; and this, among others, I felt myself.

I will just add the testimony of two of our fathers who wrote to me soon after Giulio's death. Father Armellini says, "He was my penitent when, as quite a little child, he pursued his studies for two months at our 'Convitto dei nobili,' and then again when he returned to Rome and was under private tuition in his father's house, and also during his military life as a Pontifical Zouave. He frequented the Sacraments with a piety and constancy which edified me exceedingly. I always admired in him a modesty and delicacy of conscience which is seldom to be found in young men of his temperament. He possessed the clearest light in matters relating to his soul, and he manifested them with the greatest sincerity. He was more profoundly religious than could be supposed in one so young; and he was free from all human respect. He professed what he felt, and he felt in everything as a Christian youth ought to feel. When he returned to Rome to enrol himself among the Zouaves, I was surprised to find him just as good as he used to be when I knew him as a child. The change of places and companions had made no alteration in his religious life. Just before leaving for Mentana, he desired to come from the Castle to the Gesu to make his confession; he was not permitted to pass over the bridge, and he therefore confessed to some priest whom I do not know. But although I cannot relate the circumstances which accompanied the last hours of his life, yet from what I knew of his conscience, I am certain that that last day was on his part an heroic 'act of religion,' while on the part of God it was the greatest of His gifts to that happy soul: *Raptus est ne malitia mutaret intellectum ejus.*"

Father Blosi, who was his confessor sometimes when Father Armellini was otherwise engaged, adds, "I had the good fortune to know him from the time that he presented himself at my Confessional. What devotion, what outward composure, what humility! Those who were standing round beheld with the greatest edification this holy youth kneeling at my feet without any human respect. What faith! what compunction! I think indeed that when his most beautiful soul rose to its Creator *pro Petri Sede*, his angel guardian, from whom it derived its beauty, received it and presented it to the Divine Mother, to whom he was so devoted."

Finally, Wilfrid, without being afraid of allowing his affections to lead him astray, told me more than once that he had never known any other youth with a piety so deep as his brother's; and that in these last months he seemed more than ever given to God.

And so, in the beautiful chain of God's graces and of a faithful correspondence with them which make up a virtuous life, it seemes that in Giulio's life there were three golden rings, each more resplendent than the last, of a sensible growth in piety and fervour, first at Ushaw, then at Ajaccio, and lastly at Rome.

For all let God be praised!

CHAPTER IX.

Giulio's Last Days and the Presentiment of His Death.

I WILL not now describe those celebrated days in which the hand of God was so manifestly seen in favour of Rome; but I will speak only of Giulio: I shall merely transcribe a letter in which he, in a few hurried lines written from Rome, gives his father a report of facts, and chiefly those connected with Nerola.

"October 23rd, 1867.

"MY DEAR PAPA

"We came back four days ago; six days before that we started in the train to Monte Rotondo; from thence we marched to the town, and there we slept on the straw with our sacks for pillows. This morning at half-past four we marched off to Monte Libretti; nine hours' march. Next morning at six we started for Nerola, where we heard that 1200 Garibaldians were fortified. We arrived about three o'clock in the afternoon and began the attack. Our Company was complimented on its gallantry: numbers of balls were whizzing about us: but, thanks to our Blessed Lady, we were not touched. We got into some houses and shot away at the Garibaldians from some windows: in about one hour and a half there were about seven flags of truce hanging out of the windows, and the order was given to cease firing. The cannon knocked down the flag at the third shot; and then the Pope's flag was put upon the top of the fort, and everybody shouted 'Viva Pio Nono!' It was awfully grand. We slept at Nerola in the same room with a dead soldier of the Antibe Legion; we all of us said a *de profundis* over him. First the Dutchmen said public prayers before going to sleep, and then the English: there were five of us altogether. When we took the prisoners, there were only 137: the rest had got off the night before. Next morning we marched from Nerola to Monte Rotondo, a march of sixteen hours, with our sacks on our backs. At Nerola we ate the Colonel's (De Charette) horse which was killed: it was very good: there was nothing else to eat the whole day of that long march, fifteen hours. Pray for us, dear Papa and Ellen; we often said prayers for you whilst we were out against these brutes of Garibaldians."

No one ought to wonder at Giulio's calling the Garibaldians by this name; for they thoroughly deserved it. He gives an account of their dishonourable attempt on the night of the 22nd October, to blow up one of the barracks which they had undermined; it was one of the principal barracks, and it was a good proof of what they were willing to do in Rome, if they had had a chance: Giulio wrote the following morning, "We were under arms all night at the Fort." He then mentions his numerous occupations. "It is almost impossible to find a minute to write, but, whenever I can, I will write you long letters, giving details." He here thanks his father for the present of a revolver. "Thank you, dear Papa, for the revolver; it is the most useful thing I could have; many more of us would be killed if it were not for revolvers." After this he goes on to speak most tenderly of his brother Wilfrid. "Lately Wilfrid has had attacks of fever, and he is greatly reduced; our last march made him very thin, but he is strong enough for the service in Rome. . . . . Willy sends his love to you and Ellen, and so do I. Good bye, dear Papa."

This is the last letter Giulio wrote.

The five Englishmen of whom Giulio spoke, were himself, his brother, Daniel Shea, Oswald Cary, and George Collingridge. Daniel Shea is now a serjeant, and decorated with the golden medal; Cary and Collingridge are corporals; they have given me other particulars which Giulio did not mention.

I heard from Wilfrid that when they were marching to Nerola, and passed by the cemetery of Monte Rotondo, they looked in at the gate and said a *de profundis* for those who lay there: a few days after Giulio was laid in that very cemetery for a short time. I was also told, that after night prayers, Giulio proposed that they should say one Our Father, Hail Mary, and Salve Regina, in thanksgiving for having been preserved that day.

Moreover he said the *de profundis* for the brave soldier

who had been shot on that day, and whose body was placed for the night in the Chapel of S. Anthony, where his company passed the night. And it was Giulio who prepared the lamp, which ought to burn before the dead during the night.

At length when about eleven of them had gone to sleep, and the rest were stretched on the floor to take a little repose, Captain Thomale came in, and, addressing the thirty or forty brave men there assembled, said, that after the fatigues of the day, he did not wish to *command* any one, but he wanted twelve men of good will to keep guard for a short time against any surprise of the enemy.

The first to volunteer was Giulio. Wilfrid, who was already stricken with fever, begged him not to go; but Giulio, though always so deferential to his brother, on this occasion said to him affectionately "Oh let me go," and then ran off, feeling a higher duty calling him, and after this short guard, within two hours, he threw himself down to rest with brotherly love by Wilfrid's side.

Shea also went with Giulio.

The other two Englishmen, Collingridge and his cousin Cary were on guard, wearied in body through the fatigues of the day, but more afflicted in heart at the death of Alfred Collingridge.

And here, if I may be permitted, I will give a short account of the meeting of George Collingridge and his dying brother Alfred.

It was not later than the 6th of October when Alfred

left Rome with the company, of which he was a corporal discharging the duties of serjeant. On the 13th, he did prodigies of valour with his men before the gate of Monte Libretti. In this encounter he was wounded, and taken by the Garibaldians to Nerola, with five other Zouaves, who were also wounded. It was reported in Rome that he was killed, but that the others were wounded and taken prisoners. For four days George was in the greatest anxiety about him; but on the 18th, at the entrance of Nerola, he met Mrs. Stone, who had preceded the troops, and under a heavy fire was employed in carrying water to the wounded.

She told him that Alfred was alive, but lay severely wounded in a little church close by; and George ran at once to see him, and found him very much exhausted from several bayonet and gun-shot wounds; but no one then believed that he was so near his death. Immediately after the brave George had embraced his brother, he went with his cousin Cary and the other Zouaves to attack the Garibaldians who were gathered there. After the victory George returned to Alfred's bedside, and he found him sufficiently well to see him again; he gave him a kiss for his father, his mother, his other brothers and sisters; and two hours after the poor fellow died. "He died" (wrote the Abbé Daniel in his report to Monsignor the Chaplain General) "offering his life for the Holy Roman Church, and the Holy Father." It appears that his last days were greatly assisted by the maternal care of Mrs. Stone, and the spiritual help afforded him by Mgr. Stonor and the Abbé Daniel, from whom he received all the Sacraments, and to whom he owed the great happiness of seeing again his brother and cousin; they had scarcely tasted the brief joy of having found him, when they were required to offer him up to God. He was buried at Nerola, and a Requiem Mass was sung for him at Monte Rotondo, whither the Zouaves returned.

As I was not personally acquainted with this brave soldier of the cross, I cannot say more about him, nor indeed is this the place to do so. I know that those who did know him speak of his valour and piety with great praise; I know that he passed from the Seminary of Auteuil in Paris, where he was studying with a view to following the ecclesiastical life, to the ranks of the Pontifical Zouaves, after having consulted Mgr. de Ségur on this his new vocation; I know that he hoped to go to Heaven by the direct road of martyrdom, by dying on the battle field, as a soldier, as he had formerly wished to die, as a Priest, tending the sick. I know that, in the end, he had the grace and glory to be the first of the victims of Catholic England for the cause of the Holy See.

And now to return to Giulio. A few days before his death, on his return from the fatiguing campaign of Nerola, he was met by the Countess de Redmond, who asked him to dine in her house; and as it was Friday, she told him that being dispensed she had prepared a "meat" dinner, which she felt sure would be better for him also; but she hoped that he would come in any case, and if he wished to abstain she would immediately order fish: Giulio answered, that although he could with a good conscience take advantage of a soldier's privilege in a time of such fatigue, yet he preferred to abide by the common rule of the Church; and so, without tasting any soup, he accepted with pleasure the fare which the Countess had prepared for him. Another day the same lady saw him at Mass in the Church of S. Charles in the Corso, and she went up to him with the intention of saying something; but she perceived that he was so attentive to his prayers that she drew back, not venturing to disturb his devotions.

The days which intervened between Nerola and Mentana were by no means days of repose; they were full of apprehension and fears. So much so that, for some time, when any of the Pontifical soldiers walked in the streets of the city, they always had their muskets on their shoulders in order to be on their guard against Garibaldian assassins, who, especially on the night of the 22nd of October, performed "such prodigies of valour!" One day whilst Shea and Giulio were on guard near St. Peter's, the latter invited his friend to take a cup of coffee; on entering the café they saw two men who had all the appearance of Garibaldians. Giulio fixed his eyes on them, and then turning to his friend, said, "I don't like the look of them at all; I have got my revolver, but let us say a 'Hail Mary,' that nothing may happen."

A few days before the arrival of the French in Rome, Giulio, who was pleased at their coming to defend the Holy See, nevertheless feared that they would usurp too much the duties of the Zouaves; and being stationed at the Castle of St. Angelo, he looked with the jealousy of a soldier at the French flag which now floated by the side of the Pontifical banner. He said good humouredly to his friend Shea, "I wish I could take it down; I am afraid they come to take all the fighting out of our hands, and will do our duty." Thus from day to day he awaited the orders to march against the Garibaldian forces which were continually growing stronger.

A friend told me that Giulio, a few days before the battle, whilst sitting on his bed and amusing himself by tossing a bullet about in his hands, made this remark to him, "What a capital present this would be for Garibaldi;" but, rejoined his friend, "May not Garibaldi send one to you instead?" "So much the better," replied Giulio, "for then I hope I should go straight to Heaven."

The day before the departure for Mentana the same friend perceived that he spoke with a holy joy of the chance of fighting, just as if, instead of being about to meet death, he was going to some "Festa;" and rejoicing at the thought of such a grace, he was heard to exclaim, "That is just what Papa has sent us for, Wilfrid and me." To other friends also he gave this parting salutation,—"Good bye, I hope to meet you again in Paradise." He also told Signora Geneste that he had written for the last time to his father: he kissed her little children, and told them that he would ask our Lord always to preserve them in innocence. And when he was going away, as she was standing at the balcony to salute him for the last time, she threw him two oranges, and he gracefully acknowledged the gift by a waive of his hand, saying, "These are our last *adieux*," and she returned his salutation by the remark, "We shall meet again in Paradise;" thus she saw him go away with his musket on his shoulder, looking after him as long as she could with tears in her eyes.

The Chevalier Geneste told me that one or two days before Mentana, Giulio playfully said, "If I die you must write and tell my father of it," to which his friend replied, "May Heaven preserve me from having to deliver such sad news." "And why *sad*?" rejoined Giulio, "Do you think that Papa will be so much grieved? He will rather return thanks to God. Ellen (meaning his sister) will cry a little about it, but our Lord will comfort her!" And thus it really seems that Almighty God prepared him for his death, and even gave him, as it were, a presentiment of it, which was more than a desire or hope; thus sweetly disposing one of his chosen victims for the grace and glory of the coming sacrifice.

CHAPTER X.

The Day of The Sacrafice.

THE order, which they had been expecting, to march against the Garibaldians, was given in the Castle of St. Angelo on the night of November 2nd, and received with enthusiasm. They assembled between one and two after midnight, in the square of the castle, where I believe it is the custom to say the military Mass, which on this occasion, for some reason which I do not know, could not be celebrated. It was then, as I said in the beginning of the memoir, that Wilfrid (who, if his fever had not stopped him, would have accompanied his brother), called him and his companion Cary aside, and they repeated together those last prayers with which they parted. He recommended his brother to Cary, and said, laughing, to Giulio, that he hoped he would salute the Garibaldians for him. Giulio, full of natural and supernatural courage, appeared always happy during the march, but with a recollected and prayerful joy. When they halted, about ten o'clock, his companions told me that he did not speak much, and that they never heard from his lips those expressions of enthusiasm to which others often gave utterance, and which he himself on other occasions had often spoken. His did not appear to be a courage excited by victory, but to be one resigned to sacrifice.

They believed that the battle would end rather at Monte Rotondo than at Mentana, and so Giulio agreed with a few friends, who were separated from him in different companies, that if it pleased God, they would meet in the public square of that place after the victory.

Once during the march, Cary seeing him absorbed in prayer, in a Church, said to him, "What do you desire, Giulio?" He answered with a calm countenance, "I would have a priest near me to-day!"

Almost in the first encounter with the enemy he incurred great danger. Near the Villa Santucci, a ball knocked off his cap. To see him running with fixed bayonet, bare-headed, he looked like "an angel of vengeance." This was the expression of an eye-witness, the Chevalier Sevilla, that noble Peruvian, who was close to Giulio in the battle; and who, when he had received five wounds, gave utterance to these noble words (repeated to me by the Père de Gerlache himself, who heard them), *"Vive Pie IX.! Voilà le premier sang Peruvien, qui coule pour la defense du saint Siège!"*[5]

Others have compared the Zouaves to young lions, but the picture of "angels of vengeance," seems to me more descriptive; and, moreover, when the enemy lost their arms, or fell down wounded, they showed themselves to be angels

---

5   Behold the first Peruvian blood which flows for the defence of the Holy See.

of mercy and charity. And, in very truth, that thought of Giulio's seems to me to have been angelic; I mean his holy custom of reciting an *Ave* to the Blessed Virgin, whenever he fired, for the poor soul whom his shot might send into eternity, a practice worthy of a Crusader of the age of St. Louis, combining the holy indignation and the charity of a Christian soldier; or to follow out the same idea, emulating at once the zeal of an angel of vengeance and the tenderness of an angel guardian.

Giulio also ran another considerable risk whilst driving a party of the enemy from some rising ground, amidst a shower of balls. I was told of this by that brave Irish youth, Robert Clark (now corporal), above mentioned, who ran before Giulio along the side of a hedge, every now and then turning to point out to him a less exposed road, and seeing him in this danger, called out to him, "Come up, Julian," and he answered quite coolly, "All right," and thus they reached in safety the point which they wished to occupy. Every one knows, and the General has said it in his report, that the great difficulty was in restraining their ardour and in keeping them together. It appears that Giulio was a victim to his *extreme* bravery. Being one of the few who had reached the walls of Mentana, he was shot from a window, a ball passing through his head.

A French Zouave who was near, said that whether by accident or not, in falling he lifted up his arms in the form of a cross. He fell between Mentana and some haystacks hard by, and was the *nearest* to the gate amongst those who fell. Others were *wounded* even from a nearer place; and those two brave men Valerian D'Erp and John Moëller, were wounded *mortally*, nearer still, but did not die on the field: so Giulio appears to have died on the field, nearer to the town than any one else, and also to have been the youngest; for of those who perished none seem to have been less than eighteen.

Thus he has something singular and of his own in the glory of his sacrifice.

The great idea of sacrifice explains so many facts and consoles the Christian heart; and I believe that his tutor hit upon the truth when, writing to Giulio's father, he said, "I knew him almost as well as you did, and I look upon his death as the sacrifice of a choice victim, required by God for some purpose of mercy," and indeed the voice of so much blood cries to God, with a love far more eloquent than many prayers.

It has already been observed by many, that as before at Castelfidardo, so now at Mentana, and elsewhere, Almighty God seems to have taken to himself the choicest victims; for, without appearing to be superstitious, I can truly say that among so many who were taken, not a few were the brightest flowers.

It will be sufficient to mention the lieutenant, Arthur Guillemin, who was called by his soldiers their "angel guardian;" the sub-lieutenant, Urban de Quelen, called sometimes, not in joke, but on account of his modesty, "the Capuchin," and the two worthy brothers, the sub-lieutenant

Emanuel and the Captain Adeodatus du Fournell, who united in the same spirit of sacrifice, "in morte non sunt separati," as Father de Gerlache said, who has described in his report the Christian death of both. It is sufficient to mention the Captain de Vaux, the Marshal Charles Count Bernardini, the serjeant Rialan, lieutenant the Marquis de Quartrebarbes, and those four noble men, the Baron Valerian Van Erp, the Count Carlos D'Alcantara, John Moëller, and Antony Hüggen, who have all been honoured with burial in the Belgian College; and those three Dutch heroes, Jong, Heycamp, Crone, and their companions, of whom I read a beautiful panegyric in the *Etudes religieuses, historiques, et literaires* of Paris, in December, 1867; and other private soldiers, as Henquenet, Chevalier Tremeur, Loirant, and some others, all chosen victims, like Giulio Watts-Russell and Alfred Collingridge, all glorious heroes, whose memoirs will illuminate a page in the history of Crusaders, and would not be out of place in the "Acts of the Martyrs."

It is enough to read the official accounts of the military chaplains, and the various memoirs published in France, Belgium, and Rome, in order to see the hand of God manifested, not so much in the external liberation of Rome, as in the internal works of grace in the heroism of the sacrifice of so many chosen souls.

God has made manifest a triumph by the power of his right hand, and he has accomplished it by inspiring these brave men with Christian heroism. He has prepared, chosen, and crowned his victims, and he has rewarded in many others the preparation of soul, and the simple desire of sacrifice which were the pure gifts of his grace.

The two camps at Mentana brought forcibly before my mind the two camps of S. Ignatius, in his exercise on the two standards, the one of Lucifer, the other of Christ. The names of those happy men, who in these last engagements had the courage to sacrifice their blood and their life, not for the defence of the four quarters of the globe, but for the grand principle of "Right," for the liberty of the Church, for the Holy See, for the Vicar of Jesus Christ, for Jesus Christ Himself, their names, let us hope, are all written in the book of life, for indeed they will, and justly, remain written on the memory of Rome, and of the whole Christian world. To show his gratitude, Pius IX. has decreed that a monument shall be erected to their memory at St. Lorenzo, in the Campo Verano, and that the names of all shall be inscribed on its basement, and that above shall tower a colossal statue of S. Peter in the act of presenting to a Crusader the standard of Holy Church and the sword, with those words heard of old, in the vision of Judas Macchabæus:[6] *Accipe sanctum gladium munus a Deo in quo dejicies adversarios populi mei Israel.* This most beautiful and artistic design is said to have been suggested by Pius IX. himself. Another little memorial by the Holy Father's order will be erected at Monte Rotondo.

In the meantime, friends of the slain have placed little monuments in memory of their dear ones on the very spots where they fell; and therefore it seems to me only right

---

6   2 Macc. xv. 16.

that something should be raised to Giulio also, on that spot which was the true altar of his sacrifice, with this or a like inscription.

QUI CADDE
PUGNANDO PRO SEDE PETRI
GIULIO WATTS-RUSSELL
ZUAVO PONTIFICIO
GIOVANETTO INGLESE
D'ANNI 17 E 10 MESI
IL PIU GIOVANE
CADUTO NEL CAMPO DELLA VITTORIA
E IL PIU D'APPRESSO A MENTANA.

Translation:

Here fell
Fighting for the See of Peter
Giulio Watts-Russell
A young English
Pontifical Zouave
Aged 17 years and 10 months
The youngest who fell on the field of victory
And the nearest to Mentana.

CHAPTER XI.

Other Particulars of Giulio's Death.

THE sad news of Giulio's death was soon reported to Mrs. Stone, who, together with three Sisters of Charity, attended on the wounded; and she, not being able herself to guard the body, commended the care of it to others. But two officers were present, Captain Thomale and Captain D'Arcy, who both had a great affection for Giulio, and had therefore no need to be exhorted to a special care. I, however, have not been able to obtain very exact information of what happened to the body on that evening of the third of November. I know that the Count Theodutus de Christen and the Count Emanuel de Sabran (in whose veins runs the blood of the great knight S. Elzear and his spouse S. Delphina), went in search of it; I know that Father Legier, of the Order of Preachers, without seeing the body, received from a Zouave Giulio's little book of devotions, which he consigned to Mrs. Stone. Moreover, an officer of the Antibe Legion (I do not know whether on that evening or the following morning) when he saw the body, although he did not know the soldier's name, felt so much moved that he ventured to take his beads as an act of devotion; nevertheless, when he discovered to whom they belonged, he offered to restore them to Wilfrid.

It is far more probable that Giulio was not found on that night, because, besides the necessity of giving the first care to the wounded, it was not so easy to find him; moreover the accounts of the few who had seen him are by no means precise; and the close vicinity of Mentana, which remained during that night in the hands of the enemy, rendered it more difficult. It is certain that the day *after* (November 4th), when some of the Zouaves went in search of the bodies, bewailing and at the same time envying the fate of their companions, the body of Giulio was placed in a waggon by some one who did not know him; and it was either taken from the very spot where he fell, which was close to Mentana, or from a neighbouring spot, where perhaps it had remained for that night. The fact is, that it was found at the bottom of the waggon, under other bodies which had been heaped upon it to the number of twenty-six, twenty of which were the bodies of Zouaves. It was necessary for the waggon to make a considerable digression in the fields, but at last it arrived almost at the Cemetery of Monte Rotondo, at a very late hour; and this was the cause of the burial being deferred until the following day; for the cart remained there with its load upon it during the whole night. Some friends of Giulio, and especially Shea, went searching into several places, not for a moment imagining that the body lay at the bottom of the great waggon which he himself had driven for a considerable distance, and in which he had afterwards placed other bodies.

It was only on the morning of the following day, November 5th, when they were taking out the last, that Shea, Woodward, and Cary exclaimed with one voice, "It is poor Julian!" Then with brotherly affection they recited a prayer, and having done so, they began to express astonishment at the extraordinary flexibility of the body. But just when his friends were resolving to take special care of Giulio's body, in order that they might bury it themselves, an order arrived that the body of Serjeant Rialan should remain above ground, and that the others should be interred in a place apart; one of these was a serjeant in the artillery, the Count Bernardini; three were serjeants in the Zouaves, and two were privates, Chevalier and Giulio Watts-Russell. So these three bodies were buried in a very broad and deep trench. The friends retained for themselves some little mementos of Giulio, and threw some flowers on the grave; and then Shea, with a soldier's liberty, taking a wooden cross from a neighbouring mound, inscribed on it the name of "Julian Watts-Russell," and planted it upon the spot; and this work of piety occupied nearly the whole day.

Night had already set in when the Chevalier Geneste and a French priest arrived from Rome in a carriage which had been placed at their disposal by the Marquis Patrizi, to ask for Giulio's body. It had scarcely been buried two hours, and therefore, at his entreaty, they began again this labour of love. Signor Geneste, Mr. Woodward, and a French Zouave, set to work to dig up the body, and although the grave was four or five feet deep—for fear of injuring with their spades those which had been so recently buried—they determined, as far as possible, to do all the work with their hands. Wherefore their charitable occupation ended at a very late hour, and the body remained during that night in the Chapel of the Cemetery. On the following morning, the 6th of November, General de Courten kindly lent a carriage to Signor Geneste, in order to carry Giulio's body to Rome, and to convey that of Serjeant Rialan, which had been entrusted to him, thither at the same time.

It surely will not be displeasing to the reader, who is interested in this memoir of Giulio, if I interrupt it to say one word of this his worthy companion. They were perhaps unknown to one another in this life, though, in truth, they were very much alike both in life and in death; let us believe that they became friends in Heaven for the first time. The similarity of these two beautiful souls has been spoken of before in the edifying life of Joseph Rialan, already published in French,[7] besides which the latter has been panegyrized in the *Semaine Religieuse* (7th December, 1867), and in other Catholic papers. He was born at Ploërmel, in Brittany, in 1843, and educated at the College of San Saveur de Redon, where he took the degrees of bachelor in arts and licentiate in laws. He broke off his promising career for the priesthood to become a Zouave. *"C'etait un vrai soldat,"* said in a few words those who knew him well, *"mais aussi un vrai saint."* Rialan, like Giulio, had communicated on the two preceding days (All

---

[7] Joseph Rialan, serjeant aux Zouaves Pontificaux: par R. Gheix, Paris, Lecoffre, 1868.

Saints and All Souls) and, like the martyrs of old, they both prepared for the contest by receiving the Divine Eucharist. Rialan's death crowned a life of twenty-four years—a life very pious, chaste, and studious, and consecrated to the good of the poor, in the Society of S. Vincent de Paul, of which he had been an active member from his boyhood.

His body was placed, after a short time, in the Church of S. Agnes, outside the walls of Rome, and a notice of his death was sent by telegraph, to his family, in these eloquent words, *Après trois jours transporté à Rome—corps souple—sourir d'ange—semble dormir*. It was soon after conveyed to Ploërmel in Brittany; and there they celebrated his funeral, or rather his triumph.

The Bishop of Vannes himself pronounced the funeral oration, and there was present an assembly which comprised two hundred priests, and about eight thousand of those good Bretons who came from the surrounding places;—a sight which was in truth a grand demonstration of the spirit of Catholic France. After what I have related, we cannot wonder that those who accompanied the two bodies of Rialan and Giulio, had a feeling of reverence as if they were carrying the bodies of martyrs.

Let, then, these names which are so remarkably united with one another, be coupled together also in this memoir; for, as one of the family of Rialan wrote to me—"It is sweet to think that the memory of our good Joseph should be united with that *du petit ange de l'Angleterre.*"

The body of Rialan was placed in the Church of S. Agnes,

where they awaited it; that of Giulio was carried directly to the house of the Chevalier Geneste, in the neighbourhood of S. Mary Major. I myself saw it soon afterwards, whilst it was still wrapped in a sheet; I said a prayer for him, and indeed I may almost say I said a prayer to him. I uncovered his face, blessed him, and kissed his cold forehead in his father's name.

The morning after, when the body was laid out and embalmed, I took Wilfrid to see it. We knelt down and said a *de profundis*, and I confess that when I saw that dear body, and the tears of Wilfrid, I also felt my own heart melting, and the tears started from my eyes, so that I was obliged to do violence to myself to continue my prayer. Signor Geneste told me that, in preparing the body of Giulio, he experienced the same religious emotions, as formerly when he was discharging these pious offices for that of Joseph Guerin. In that very house Giulio had often heard Signor Geneste speak in eloquent language the praises of Guerin, the hero of Castelfidardo; and now he—Signor Geneste—spoke in the same language of this hero of Mentana. Moreover, Giulio had often kissed the medal of the ancient image of our Blessed Lady of Spoleto, which Guerin had brought from that place on his march to Castelfidardo, and which he had left with Signor Geneste, as a souvenir of his death bed; he kissed it with much affection, as he had heard that the Holy Father Pius IX. had done, when it was presented to him by Signor Geneste to be blessed. He had often heard the latter recount, with the pleasure of a friend, how much he had done for the body of Guerin, never imagining that in that very place he would do the same for himself, and that he there would receive honours as the Guerin of England. During the days on which Giulio remained exposed in that house crowds of all kinds of persons came, some from devotion, some from curiosity to see a dead body which had no appearance of a corpse, because it was so life-like and flexible in all its members. Some, indeed, not contented with gazing on him and praying by his side, kissed his hands, and took away the evergreens which surrounded him, and some even touched him with their medals and beads. The Roman correspondent of the *Westminster Gazette* thus wrote of Giulio—"The body was embalmed . . . . many went to see it, almost as to that of a martyr . . . . he had been so skilfully treated by the French surgeon that the wound did not at all disfigure his handsome face. He looked just as a boy might, whose mother had but now dressed his wound and commended him to sleep." Another eye-witness wrote—"There was a most happy smile upon his face." A young Englishman, who had been his friend, and who, up to the present time had desired to enlist as a Zouave, but had not been allowed to do so, went to see him; and his mother, as he told me, was not without some hope that the sight of his dead friend might in some degree mitigate this youthful desire; but it had exactly the opposite effect. This visit filled him with new fervour, and he told his mother that he wished at once to take Giulio's post. He immediately obtained leave, and is now a Zouave.

Thus, these two days were days of triumph; and so in fine

was the day of the funeral itself, which was solemnised in the chapel of the English College. In the Church, according to custom, the body was placed in a covered coffin; but in the afternoon it was uncovered again, in order that it might be laid in a zinc coffin, and transported to S. Lorenzo. In the meantime, I had gone into a Chapel, upstairs in the English College, to hear confessions; when two of the students came running to me, saying, "Come, father, and see Julian; how beautiful he looks." I know that such impressions may often be owing to the affection of friends, but I must confess that his countenance and the smile on his face seemed to me to be more than ordinarily joyous and happy. Every one looked at him with pleasure, though his face was necessarily a good deal marred by his wounds. He had only one eye remaining, and part of his forehead was terribly bruised and burnt by the gun-powder. He had no longer the adornment of white roses, of the palm, or the crucifix, or the scapular, or the Zouave uniform in which he was laid out in the church; all that was to be seen was a dead body, dressed in white, embalmed certainly, but not until four days after death, and after it had been carried from Mentana to Monte Rotondo, under the pressure of other dead bodies, buried without any coffin, then disinterred, and carried to Rome, covered only slightly with a sheet. Giulio had often, when conversing, an ingenuous and attractive smile, but the ordinary expression of his face was collected and grave; I should say indeed distinguished by a thoughtfulness beyond his years, as may be seen in his photograph; and now that face so disfigured with the wound and the blood, and the earth, and shaken by rough journeys, was so fresh and joyous, that, without poetical exaggeration, I may apply to it those words, "This beautiful death appears in his beautiful face." But above all it was impossible not to wonder at the freshness and flexibility of his limbs; so that some lifted his head from the pillow on which it rested, and some his arms and his hands, as if they belonged to a living person, who was asleep.

Now, without seeking to see in all this anything supernatural, I am content to say that it was most consoling; and so I will finish with the words of two young men, by no means devotees, who, as has been mentioned before, went to the house of Signor Geneste to see him, and satisfy their curiosity, and who were heard to say to one another with an air of wonderment, "Non possiam chiuder gli occhi all'evidenza del fatto." We cannot shut our eyes to the evidence of the fact.

CHAPTER XII.

Marks of Esteem and Affection shown towards Giulio after Death.

THE extraordinary freshness of the body, which excited the tender feelings of those who saw it, appears to me to be a figure of his beautiful death, which was precious both in the sight of men and angels, and which moved the hearts of many even to tears; for thus our Lord is pleased to glorify, even on earth, as it seems best to Him, those whom He rewards in Heaven. Other noble victims of this last crusade had a more splendid triumph, which enhanced the greatness of their name or raised their military renown; but this young hero, merely on account of his tender age and his singular virtues, without anything remarkable about him, is invested, as it were, with a heavenly mantle, which moves our hearts to tenderness and devotion. His funeral was not magnificent; but among so many persons present, there was not one whose heart was cold and absent. Those obsequies in the English College were celebrated, so to say, as if all the spectators were of one family. The Mass was sung by the Rector, Father

O'Callaghan. He moreover, wished that Wilfrid, on account of his health, should pass these days in the College; which was a great pleasure to all the students, and to those especially who had been companions of Wilfrid and Giulio at Ushaw College, in England. These latter accompanied the body to the cemetery, following the carriage in which I, Mr. Geneste, and Wilfrid were reciting the Office of the Dead. Other students and friends had preceded us; and when, before closing the grave, Wilfrid knelt down for the last time to place on the coffin of his beloved brother two garlands of flowers gathered in the Pope's garden, all eyes were fixed upon him, and there was an eloquent silence which made evident the emotion of the bystanders, even strangers, who were gathered there. I was also deeply affected by being near the grave of my dear friend, General Tylee, and by the memory of a young man whom I had laid in the same cemetery, although in another part; I allude to Albert Atlee, of whom I delight to speak as "The Benjamin" of my dear English converts, and of whom it would be a pleasure to me to write another edifying memoir. For, seeing that he came to Rome in search of bodily health, to his great happiness he found in its stead health of soul by becoming a Catholic, and he died one of the most beautiful deaths which I have ever had the happiness to witness; and what increases my joy is the conversion of his mother and his sisters, now fervent Catholics.

The idea of writing these events was suggested to me in a consoling conversation with Wilfrid on my return from the cemetery. At the first I wrote a letter to the Cavaliere

Mencacci, editor of the *Divin Salvatore*, which was published by itself, and afterwards reprinted in a separate form, and translated into English, French, and German; so that it carried the name of Giulio far and wide, and won for him a place in the hearts of multitudes; for which reason I have left it in its original form at the beginning of this biography; and I thank God that I have been able to write these few words upon a subject so attractive, to His greater glory and that of His youthful servant.

I am emboldened to say that the Holy Father, Pope Pius IX., condescended to hear it read to him at full length, and on that occasion expressed how much he felt in words of heart-felt sympathy; blessing, through love for Giulio, the whole family of Watts-Russell. May the blood of Giulio and the benediction of the Holy Father ever call down in all its fulness the Divine Mercy upon all his relatives, whether Catholic or Protestant. Meanwhile, in Rome, the name of Giulio spread more and more, and three things especially were in everybody's mouth, the extraordinary flexibility of the body, his words to Wilfrid after a moment of anger, when he fell upon his knees and made an act of contrition, and gave him his hand, and above all the motto—

"Anima mia, anima mia,
Ama Dio e tira via."

Among others, Dr. Neve, formerly Rector of the English College, told me that he was astonished to hear this little verse repeated on all sides as a proverb; and even I, several months later, have heard some, who either did not recollect or could not pronounce the name Watts-Russell, use in its place this beautiful paraphrase: "Il Zuavetto Inglese Anima mia."

Not in Rome only, but in all the places which Giulio had visited and they were many in England, France, Italy, Corsica, and Germany—everywhere the notice of his death called forth the esteem and love felt for him, with a tenderness which had something remarkable about it. One letter from Ushaw said, "When the news of his death came, it sent a thrill to every heart." In another occur these words, "It was not that we grudged dear Giulio his martyr's crown; still one could not refrain from tears . . . . but do we not repeat in Blessed Stephen's office, that holy men *fecerunt planctum magnum super eum*? and yet they doubted not of his being with Jesus, as holy Church's most glorious martyr." Another letter from a Carmelite Nun at Darlington, where Giulio was well known, from his having stayed for some time on a visit to the Chaplain of the house, says, "How happy we are and greatly privileged to have known our young English martyr . . . . you cannot form an idea with what affection and veneration that gallant boy's name is enshrined in the hearts of Carmel's inmates." And again, "The emotions which the tidings of his glorious death caused at Carmel I cannot describe; tears of joy and yet of regret for the gallant boy flowed on all sides; and no brother could have been more tenderly mourned for than was that valiant child." A Religious gave to Giulio's father and sister, in the name of the community, a small picture of the field of Mentana, in which that town is represented in the distance, and Giulio's soul as winging its flight from the field of battle to Our Lady, by her to be presented to her Divine Son. His grave is adorned with lilies and forget-me-nots, the first a type of himself, the latter of those left who love him on earth. Another letter says, "The account of his death drew tears from our eyes." Out of love for his memory Masses of the dead were celebrated in the places where he was known, and, just as before in the English College at Rome, so these funeral ceremonies had something in them of festive devotion.

I will not mention the affectionate words which were written to me of Giulio by Father Kenelm Digby Beste, of the Oratory of S. Philip Neri, in London, who knew him almost from a child; but I will content myself with giving an extract from an eloquent lecture delivered by him to the Brothers of the little Oratory, and published under the title of "Victories of Rome," where, after having spoken of the sweet sacrifice of his innocent young life, he thus affectionately salutes him: "God bless thee, Julius Watts-Russell. When last we saw thee thou wert but a child, delighting to play in S. Philip's house and garden; and now, with glorious palm, thou art already a stately martyr, amidst the white-robed host of Paradise."

I hope that I shall not displease the Rev. W. Tylee, cousin of the General already mentioned, if I take the liberty of recording certain extracts from two letters, in which, with the confidence of a friend, he thus opens his heart to me—"I have been beyond everything edified and gladdened by the glorious death of our two noble Zouaves, especially Julian Russell, for I knew him and shall always value the great honour of his acquaintance to the end of my life; he was a real soldier of Jesus Christ, and a martyr for his holy cause. He gave me (as also Wilfrid) his photograph in his Zouave dress, before I left Rome. I have had it set and framed with your inscription illuminated, *ad martyrum cryptas*, and put over my reading table with the text, *Beati mundo corde*, underneath . . . . . I am so glad that the good General and Julian are sleeping side by side; it will make my next visit to S. Lorenzo doubly interesting . . . . I wrote to Wilfrid to congratulate him on Julian's death, as I said I could not condole with him."

If I may be permitted, I will give another extract; since this little biography is due to Mr. Tylee, as I should never have written it had it not been for his offer to translate into English those letters which I had published in the *Divin Salvatore*, and which appeared under the title of *Memoirs of Giulio*. "And now," so he wrote to me, "I am going to ask your leave to translate the little book about Julian. It will be a labour of love, and it may be good that those who cannot read Italian should be able to learn more about this noble and holy youth; of course I should not put my name to it, but call myself the translator." But I thought it better to extend the former memoir into this biography; and had it not been for so many pressing occupations which obliged me to postpone it first to the Easter Vacation, and then to Whitsuntide, I should be ashamed now to have reached the feast of S. Peter without having finished it to him therefore I joyfully offer this brief eulogy upon his Crusader, which it has been a labour of love or rather a *recreation of love* for me to write.

As then I have not hesitated to publish my own name, and the names of Giulio's relations and friends, so neither do I wish to omit the name of Mr. Tylee; and I desire that in this biography, together with the dear name of Giulio, shall be united the names of the poor author and translator. Moreover I beg of him that he will faithfully translate these words as if he were writing them of somebody else.

Now to turn again to the testimonies of affectionate esteem for Giulio. The same Mr. Tylee, writing to his friend the Rev. P. Sweeny at the Pio College, says, "I cannot tell you how that noble boy's death has affected me; there was something engaging in him, so unlike what one sees in other boys. There was the refinement and grace of this world, as well as that sweetness which is alone the work of the Holy Ghost."

A priest who made Giulio's acquaintance by chance, on his last journey to Rome, and became very intimate with him, thus wrote to a friend:—"Even for the short time that I had his company on the way to Rome I was again and again struck by his fine, frank, single-hearted, generous disposition and manners, and could not but have an affection and esteem for him; and as upon his part there was a return of great kindness and confidence I was soon upon terms of friendship with him, and felt just as affectionate and warm towards him as if I had been intimate with him for years . . . . You may imagine then what a bitter grief and wound to my natural feelings were the tidings of his death. Having had such a love for him I could not restrain my grief and tears, and often and often the thought of him has since absorbed my mind almost unconsciously." "It is poor weak nature," he says; but I would rather say that it was the grace of God, which so softened his heart for the honour of Giulio's memory, and perhaps also to recompense the fortitude of the father who appeared to make the sacrifice with dry eyes.

Don Liberato, his tutor, wrote to me—"If God spares my life to visit again the shrine of S. Peter, I will at the same time visit the tomb of his young Crusader; I am certain that he will look kindly from Heaven upon his relations and friends. O Adolescens Christi Miles, vive in Deo."

Mr. Langdon, a friend of the family, calls Giulio "our dear and happy young martyr," and he adds, "it is quite a luxury to look at the face of that dear boy, even in his photograph." The Canon Forcioli, who knew him and loved him so well in Ajaccio, gave away several copies of the first memoir which I published, and, by the advice of the Bishop of Ajaccio, he desired that it should be reprinted by hundreds and distributed all over Corsica.

M. Louis Veuillot having asked for information from the parents of any Zouaves who had fallen thus wrote to Mr. Watts-Russell when he had received the little memoir of Giulio: *"Elle sera au nombre des meilleurs ornements, du livre que je me propose d'écrire;"* he says also, *"Si j'avais un fils à donner, je le donnerais, et j'envierais pour lui le sort de votre cher martyr."*[8]

---

8   It will be among the number of the finest ornaments of the book which I

Don Joseph Calderan, Giulio's tutor when at Venice, and godfather in Confirmation, writes thus: "When I saw the name of Giulio on the title-page of the article my heart was touched, and the thought immediately suggested itself, 'then my Giulio is a martyr and an angel in Heaven;' and when I had read the brief account how he had been a worthy victim in the cause of God, I shed tears of consolation, as did also the Carmelite Fathers at Venice, and many other persons who had the happiness of knowing him when he was a child, and could not cease to love him after he grew up." Also in writing to his father, he says, "Since I wish to express frankly the real sentiments of my heart, I must say that I should consider that I insulted the memory of my dear and heroic Giulio if I approached you with words of condolence. Allow me to grasp your hand and congratulate you on having such a son."

I know that Mr. Watts-Russell has received many letters of this kind, and if he was in Rome, I could perhaps prevail on his modesty so far as to obtain some extracts from them; but indeed I can select more than enough from the various letters which I myself have received, both from France and Germany, from persons with whom I was not acquainted, but who had read the memoir of Giulio. Nor will I hesitate to do so from a puerile fear lest any should say that I wish to laud myself for nothing at all while praising Giulio. My subject was my success; and I ought to say, to the glory of Giulio, that even the gravest people told me that they could not restrain their tears for this youth, whom they never even

---

purpose writing. If I had a son to give I would have given him, and I should desire for him the lot of your dear martyr.

knew personally, and they thanked me for having given, in this little book, as it were, a photograph of Giulio, which drew the hearts and esteem of everyone by the mere sight of it. One person wrote to me, "I have read it and re-read it, and always with pleasure . . . . It was not the *Chassepôts* which worked these prodigies, but such souls as Giulio Watts-Russell." Another said, "It is difficult to decide which is better, peace, or war like this conducted by such heroes." Another wrote to me thus, "What a beautiful life was that of Giulio, what a beautiful death!" Some have even taken Giulio's prayers, which are added at the end of the memoir, and have recited them with their daily prayers.

A French Priest wrote and told me that he had wished to read from the pulpit during the *Month of Mary*, various extracts from the memoir of Giulio, especially to give an example of the power of devotion to the most holy Virgin in a young soul (*un exemple de ce que peut sur une jeune âme la dévotion envers la Ste Vierge*).

One of our fathers at Caserma in the Brazils wrote me word that he had read the memoir to the young lay students in the College, during the month of May, to their great edification and delight.

Above all, several Bishops have caused it to be circulated in their Seminaries, with an admonition that he could be held up as an example not only to soldiers, but even to ecclesiastics. In fine, in the letters which I have received, all have spoken of Giulio with tenderness and affection, and I will say even with devotion, and many have called him a young

Saint in his life, and a Martyr in his death. It is not because I like to speak hyperbolically that I have given to Giulio the name of "Martyr;" for in some sense it seems to me that I have reason to call him so, since, on the one side, it is certain that he offered himself on the battlefield for the sole motive of religion, and on the other, on the part of the revolutionists, the war was waged and animated by a spirit of irreligion, more than by a false spirit of nationality; wherefore in the Zouave, they did not hate so much an enemy in the field as the Catholic defenders of Rome.

For myself, though I have made some prayers for Giulio, and taken part in his obsequies, I wish to confess with sincerity that I have never said one *Mass of Requiem* for him. I know that there is a cruel piety, which arises from a too great esteem for those whom we hold dear; but in this case, after such a life and such a death, I hope that my heart will not have betrayed me, and that the great esteem in which Giulio was held by so many, may not be an exaggeration, and an illusion of exalted minds, but rather an enthusiasm of those who possess a mind and heart, which can appreciate the beautiful sacrifice of a chosen victim.

A short time after Giulio's death, the following was written from Ushaw: "The enthusiasm at Ushaw is very great . . . Julian's photographs are amongst us. I fancy a couple of hundred will be amongst us next week. Two young fellows, who had given up studying for the Church, left here yesterday with the intention of starting for Rome." In another letter it was stated that the Ushaw boys were asked for some prizes for a raffle, to provide the necessary outfit for some men who were about to enlist as Zouaves. "On one day three hundred (mostly very valuable) prizes were given; the boys stripping themselves of everything they had got which they prized, gold pins, College prizes, prayer books, and so on."

These words closed an article which appeared in the *Westminster Gazette* of December 7th: "Ushaw students may indeed feel proud that S. Cuthbert has sent forth so glorious a son, and exclaim in their hearts, May our end be like unto his! May many more from Ushaw, Oscott, Stonyhurst, and Old Hall have the honour to fight and die for so glorious a cause!"

In very truth, from these and other Colleges, and many parts of England, have come forth young men to join the Pope's Army. I will not name anyone; I will only say that I know other Watts-Russells; and I will merely add what Mgr. Stonor said to me about one of these who is very dear to me, and was a personal friend of Giulio's. After praising this young Zouave, who at that time, on account of severe illness, was obliged to go away on sick leave, he ended by saying generally, "certainly the English and Irish set that we have are most edifying. How far these young men were influenced by the good example of Giulio Watts-Russell, I cannot say, but I am not astonished at seeing that Giulio with his maxim,

"Ama Dio e tira via,"

has had no small influence, especially on those noble Zouaves who came from Canada. The motto

"Aime Dieu et va ton chemin," of Giulio, was proposed and adopted in council as the most appropriate for the expedition; and it was embroidered in red letters under the arms of Canada, which, together with the Pontifical arms, were displayed on their banner; whence it seems to me that Giulio can be called the standard-bearer of this little legion, I might almost say, of angels sent by God so unexpectedly for the succour of Catholic Rome.

With this banner displayed, more than one hundred and fifty Canadian youths departed from Montreal with the benediction of their Bishop, and amid the acclamations of the people. During their long journey they encouraged one another with this motto, *Aime Dieu et va ton chemin*, with this banner held on high, they all went in a body to visit the churches in Paris, and other cities. With this displayed, on the tenth of March they entered Rome, and marched to the Basilica of the Prince of the Apostles. And indeed I know not whether these young men were more struck with wonder at that grand church on this their first visit to it, or the Romans at beholding so unusual a spectacle. Certain it is that Canada has been a subject of amazement to Rome and to the world; and I was well pleased with the *naïve* remark of a simple-hearted Roman, who saw these three hundred young men entering the Basilica; shaking his head he exclaimed—"A hundred years hence they will find it difficult to believe what we now witness; it appears like a romance."

This richly embroidered banner, and the motto of the English Zouave which it bore were very much talked of in

The banner of the Canadian Papal Zouaves

Rome. Moreover I, through the courtesy of the Abbé Moreau, chaplain of the Canadian regiment, was able to examine it at my leisure; and, although I was assured that the motto was taken from Giulio, I had some little doubt about it, because one of the Canadians had told me that this motto (now embroidered in red) was the dying exclamation of a Crusader, which he wrote with his blood; from which information I suspected that report, *quæ vires acquirit eundo*, had exaggerated my simple statement, that these were the last words written in Italian, in Giulio's book! Perhaps some one may have said (speaking figuratively) that Giulio had sealed these words with his blood; and so it came to be imagined that he had really written them with his blood, on the field of Mentana. The Canadians were persuaded of the truth of my conjectures, and they all assured me that the motto was Giulio Watts-Russell's. Nevertheless to make the matter certain, I wrote to Doctor Chandonnet, director of the Normal School of Laval, and this beautiful answer was returned from Quebec: *"Oui; le motto de la bannière Canadienne est celui de Giulio Watts-Russell. Oui, son nom est venu jusqu'à nous, et son exemple a contribué, j'en suis sur, à attirer les cœurs à Dieu. Dites le sans crainte."** He then goes on as follows:—"At Mentana we had already two of our young countrymen, Hugh Murray and Alfred Larocque; they were wounded, and the sight of their noble blood inflamed our courage. We are Catholics, and we love our Father. His cause is more than our own; it is also that of our brothers, and it is the cause of God. And did not the misfortunes, which have lately visited us, still exist, we should have maintained a thousand brave men around the rock of S. Peter." Finally, he returned thanks to me for the short memoir which I had written, and which I never thought would have caused the Crusaders of Canada to make Giulio's motto their own.

After this I can end my little biography as I began it; among the glorious victims of Mentana, one of the most renowned was the young Pontifical Zouave, Giulio Watts-Russell. And I can add that not the family of Watts-Russell only, but also "Catholic England may well glory in his death," as a lady of Nantes (that city so famous in the history of the Zouaves), expressed herself to me. Truly (as I have already stated), if other Zouaves had a more splendid outward triumph, of Giulio it may be said, in no ordinary degree, that an affection more tender, more universal, and I will say more devoted, was awakened towards him to attract souls to God. It seems that the sacrifice of this young Zouave was not only most pleasing to God, but that He delighted in it, and that the good odour of its sweetness was spread abroad to the edification of many. This is the best consolation in their loss, for those who loved him so deeply.

His Aunt, the Baroness Martini, thus wrote to the Count Vimercati: "God has given him the grace to sacrifice his life for a holy cause; and it was done in a spirit of profound piety. In this is our glory—our consolation. May the Lord grant that he may intercede for his family, who loved him with such affection."

In this most Christian spirit, the same Baroness Martini, and the Countess de Montgelas, also Giulio's Aunt, wrote to me, and also other relations and friends.

And now, last of all, addressing myself to Giulio's father, brother, and all his relations, and to the head of the family, Mr. Watts-Russell, Giulio's grandfather, I will say not one word of condolence, but only of Christian congratulation.

Giulio's death was not a misfortune to his family, but a grace and a glory.

Let us then return thanks to God, to Whom we owe this grace and the glory of this sacrifice.

With all my heart, I offer my congratulations, but more especially to you, my dearest Giulio, happy Crusader of S. Peter, valiant Soldier of Christ.

Adolescens Christi miles
Vive in Deo.

CHAPTER XIII.

Giulio's Father.

IT has been felt that the second edition of this little book could not be complete without a few words about Julian's father, who has been so often mentioned in these pages. The writer of this chapter, who had the great privilege of his friendship, can truly say that he was a man who lived for God alone. He was one of those favoured men who give up all that the world holds dear for Christ's sake.

At the very beginning of what is called the Oxford movement, he, together with his great friend Father Faber, resigned his living in Northamptonshire, which was near one of his father's estates, in order to enter the true Church of God; and though, after his wife's death, for a very considerable time he remained a layman, he at last fulfilled his earnest desire to serve God at His holy Altar, and though he was advanced in life, he offered himself for the sacred ministry and was accepted.

He was ordained priest at St. Mary's, Clapham, in the year

1868, and for the last seven years of his life had the great privilege of offering daily the holy Sacrifice of the Mass. His intense love for the holy Mother of God determined him to make Lourdes his home, though his duties to his children caused him to leave the blessed Sanctuary from time to time. He, however, had the great privilege of dying at his favourite shrine, after a short illness—indeed so short, that his son, Father Michael, could not reach Lourdes in time to see his father alive.

So great was his humility that he insisted on being laid on the floor to receive the Sacrament of Extreme Unction.

He died on the Feast of S. Gabriel, the 18th of March, 1875, on the Eve of S. Joseph, the patron of a holy death.

His name was so much venerated in the little town of Lourdes, that two thousand people followed him to his grave.

The writer of this chapter remembers with great edification his unflinching faith—the doctrines and practices of the Church were indeed part of his life.

The chilling atmosphere of Protestantism in England only stimulated more than ever his thorough Catholicism.

He longed for the return of his country to the obedience of the Supreme Pontiff, and he wrote a beautiful prayer[9] with this intention, to the devout repetition of which H.E. the Cardinal Archbishop of Westminster has lately attached an Indulgence at the request of his son, Father Michael. The love of God which burnt in his heart showed itself in his charity

---

9   This prayer will be found at the end of the book.

towards the poor, and this to such an extent, that he would often send out from his own table a considerable portion of his dinner to feed some hungry fellow creature who asked his alms. I may say truly that his practice of the supernatural virtues made him a model to many Catholics, and especially to some converts who forget that the singular grace which they have received from God requires a singular return of correspondence.

The translator cannot conclude without saying, that he hopes it will please God to bless the second edition of this little book, though 23 years have elapsed since it was first published.

Its lessons are obvious. This young soldier of Christ laid down his life for the independence, or in other words, the temporal sovereignty of the Vicar of Jesus Christ. We are all too apt to forget the past and to take things as they are; because twenty years have elapsed since the Piedmontese took possession of the States of the Church, they are no more entitled to them than they were on the first day on which they entered Rome. The protests of our Holy Father, Leo XIII., against this unjust and sacrilegious usurpation, are quite as vehement and continued as the protests of his predecessor. He holds this property in trust for the Roman Church as the Patrimony of the Prince of the Apostles Himself. Accordingly the words of his predecessor are practically always repeated by the reigning Pontiff, "non possumus;" *i.e.*, "We cannot condone sacrilege," we cannot resign what the Providence of God has committed to our keeping.

APPENDIX.

Giulio's book of Devotions.
A visit to his tomb.

AS a complement and crown of this memoir, I could add some beautiful extracts from his manuscript book of devotions; his daily prayer for the conversion of England, for her Queen, intentions in the Holy Mass for his family, the prayer to the most sacred Heart of Jesus; but I fear that I must content myself with those three prayers only of which I have made express mention in this memoir. The first prayer, to be used for anyone who retains even a spark of devotion to Our Lady, is piously believed to be the composition of S. Germaine Cousin. The second, in old and quaint English, is by a saintly Nun, Mother Margaret Mostyn, a member of an old Catholic family in Wales. She entered a Carmelite convent in Belgium, in the time of the Protector Cromwell, and the community afterwards fled into England, when the French Revolution broke out. She died in the odour of sanctity, and is considered by the Carmelite Nuns at Darlington almost as their foundress. This act of homage to the Blessed Virgin, which was so often on Giulio's lips, is now in his hands, in the grave. The third is the English version of the popular Spanish hymn, in honour of the most Holy Trinity. As I said before, Giulio learnt this from me, and I learnt it from the good General Tylee, near to whose monument I caused the grave of Giulio to be made; and they are sleeping side by side, *"ad cryptas Martyrum,"* the old and the young soldier of Christ. But besides these (which I mentioned in my first memoir), I ought now gratefully to add an Italian Poem, entitled "Una visita al sepolcro di Giulio," which is a very jewel of devotion: I received it by letter anonymously, from some gentleman, who, although his only acquaintance with Giulio was through my short memoir, nevertheless has written with the affection and feeling of an intimate friend.

I.

O Marie! Obtenez, je vous en conjure, pour toutes les âmes qui auront encore conservé au fond de leurs coeurs la moindre étincelle d'amour pour vous, le moindre souvenir de vous dans leurs esprits, obtenez que leurs chaines soient brisées, et qu'elles soient preservées de la mort éternelle. Amen.

II.

O thou most glorious, most Immaculate, and perpetual Virgin Mary, the Mother of my God, I vow myself to continue thy most humble and devoted servant . . . . I promise that I will frequently reverence thee and ever love and invoke thee, and I will rejoice that I may serve thee, from this instant, till the last hour and moment of my death. *Control then at that time all those wicked spirits*, which may be then either breeding idle fancies in my head, or preparing dangerous snares for my feet, that by thy intercession and protection which can never be wanting, when it is sought, I may one day and for ever adore the God of Majesty, in his Holy Court of Heaven, under thy mantle, and at thy feet; and for the present I have the purpose, and raise it so far as to be a promise, that I will daily ask thy blessing more than once, and it shall be my first act in the morning, and my last in the evening; and, if I may without note, I will also kiss the ground at the same time. I will also give every day some little alms, either corporal to some poor distressed creature, or spiritual, to the souls in Purgatory, in memory and in honour of thee, to the end, that at my death thou mayest give me the goodness of an eternal happy life at thy feet; and I will procure to carry this protestation about me, both living and dying, so that it will *be found about my person*, and I desire also that it may be buried with me, as a testimony of defiance against all the devils in hell, and of the hearty hope that I have, and will ever have, in thy prayers and protection, O thou Holy Queen of Heaven, the Mother of my God, and of me. In the meantime every Saturday I will read upon my knees the copy of this protestation, that so I may be often renewing the memory of thy presence, and that as I am joyed in meditating diligently upon thee, thou also mayest be pleased to take continual care of my poor soul.

III.

Blessed and praised be the most Holy Trinity,
    Father, Son, and Holy Ghost.
Holy, Holy, Holy, Lord God of Hosts,
    Full are the heavens and earth
    Of the Majesty of thy glory.
    Glory to the Father,
    Glory to the Son,
    Glory to the Holy Ghost.
I believe in the most Holy Trinity!
I hope in the most Holy Trinity!
I love the most Holy Trinity!
I am sorry for having offended the most Holy Trinity!
I desire to see the most Holy Trinity.
Amen.

IV.

Adolescens Christi miles
Vive in Deo.

Lessi Giulio di te—parole scritte
Da un uom di Dio che ti connobe e piansi.
Le tue virtù vi lessi, e il sacrificio
Di tua giovine vita alla più santa
Delle cause terrene e in un divina.
Del genitor, della sorella il duolo

Rassegnato vi lessi, e di Vilfrido
La fraterna pietà.—Lessi dei molti
Amici il lutto, et dei compagni Eroi,
Invidi nobilmente e desiosi
Di tua morte sublime, il vale estremo.

Gloria ai Prodi immortal! per voi l'eterna
Città fu salva, e per voi salvo il Padre
Delle Cristiane genti. Il secol nostro
Ha i suoi martiri anch'esso e fra le donne
Le sue Prassedi. Breve stuol ne vedo
Aggirarsi pel campo e dei caduti
Non scevrar le divise, e il pio conforto
Dar d'una voce e d'una mano amica.
In te s'imbatte alcuna, a cui sei noto!
Ti solleva; ti guarda—è fermo è muto
Il tuo cuor generoso! alla famiglia
Pensa la Pia gemendo, e il caro pegno
Fa porre in salvo. Oh benedetta! il Cielo
D'altri pietosi Ti rimerti per lei.
La carità seccede, e Roma accoglie
La gloriosa salma—alle sue membra,
Mobili come vive, i vestimenti
Si rendon del guerrier.—La fronte offesa
Di bianche rose inghirlandata asconde
La ferita crudel;—la palma in l'una
Nell'altra mano il Crocifisso; al seno
Tien di Maria l'immago. "In questa forma
Giace il bel giovinetto e par che dorma"

Giulio Watts-Russell — 1868.

Venne il Padre da lunge, e di vederlo
Nel dischiuso sepolcro ebbe la forza.
Lo rivider la suora ed il fratello.
Scelti amici divisero con essi
La mestissima gioia. Averne anch'io
Parte ho bramato e di sua tomba al piede,
Dopo letto quel libro, andar mi piacque
Sull'ora del tramonto a salutarlo.

Giunsi e di mille tumoli
    Nel multiforme aspetto,
    Il suo conobbi al palpito
    Che mi sentii nel petto;
    All'improvvisa lagrima
    Che il ciglio mio bagnò.

Baciai devoto e supplice
    Quel sasso e quella Croce,
    Volli pregar, ma tremula
    Nol consenti la voce,
    Che della morte il cantico
    In un sospir mutò.

Dormi o Gentile.—Aleggino
    Miti qui l'aure intorno.—
    Gli astri su te risplendano
    Quando sparisce il giorno.—
    L'erbette e i fior circondino
    Il tuo modesto avel.

Campion di Christo a vivere
    Fosti chiamato in Dio.

Anche lassù recorditi
Che Roma amasti e Pio.—
Fra gli Angioli e fra i Martiri
Prega per loro in ciel.

Prayer for the Conversion of England, specially indulgenced by HIS EMINENCE CARDINAL MANNING, *Feast of St. Edward, 1890 .*

Prayer for the Conversion of England, specially indulgenced by HIS EMINENCE CARDINAL MANNING, Feast of St. Edward, 1890.

HOLY and glorious Saints of England! Holy Kings and Queens, Bishops, Priests and Religious, Virgins, Martyrs, Confessors and Solitaries, All ye, who by your lives of suffering have won for this land the glorious title of the "Dowry of Mary," look down with pity upon its present desolation, behold its ruined churches, its desecrated shrines, its departed glory; think upon the sacred spots where you have lived and laboured, and poured out your blood for God's honour; revisit the places where your very names are forgotten and where your holy relics are still lying dishonoured and unknown. Pray for us, Holy Saints, that we may live unto God, that we may love again the Mother of God, that we may be loyal and devoted children of the Vicar of Christ, so that England may again become a joy upon earth, and by the ardour of her zeal and the generosity of her love for God, she may be able to make some poor amends for all her past ingratitude and betrayal of the Truth. AMEN.

"*An indulgence of 50 (fifty) days is granted to all who devoutly use this prayer.*"

HENRY EDWARD,
Cardinal Archbishop.

GIULIO WATTS-RUSSELL

Twenty-Seven Years After His Death

A SEQUAL TO HIS BIOGRAPHY

BY THE LATE

CLAUD R. LINDSAY
A.M.D.G.

ORIGINALLY PUBLISHED IN 1895 BY

LONDON:
ART AND BOOK COMPANY
AND LEAMINGTON

INTRODUCTION.

THE events that have occurred this year in connection with Julian Watts-Russell, Pontifical Zouave, who fell in the Battle of Mentana, have been of so remarkable a character, as almost to force one to see in them the hand of Providence, acting in an especial manner to revive in hearts and minds the memory and admiration of one the like of whom has, perhaps, seldom been met with, and to place him prominently before our eyes as a model of what a true Christian and loyal son of the Church should be and feel.

In these days of deplorable tepidity, and even error, among Catholics, in regard to what is called the Roman Question, it is good to have such a model to point to. The study of a life and death like Giulio's is worth all the arguments in the world, no matter how valid and convincing they may be. It is a story that teaches us that the shedding of one's blood for the temporal sovereignty of the Pope is not only a pleasing sacrifice in the eyes of God, but also a signal grace from Him—a grace given in recompense for sanctity of life. Not that all who fell fighting for the See of Peter were saints; but I have small hesitation in affirming that, with those who offered themselves and their lives in defence of this cause, from pure motives of true love of God and His Church—and they were not few who were so animated—it would be found, if their biographies were read, that their death was the crowning act of lives of sanctity and faithful service, in which generosity to God was the key-note.

No impartial reader can fail to see that Giulio's death was the reward of his life—that it was a great grace merited by a correspondence to previous graces almost angelic, his wonderful and, indeed, touching devotion to our Blessed Lady, his charity to the poor, and his other virtues. It is as apparent as it can be, and no keenness of perception is required to discover it.

This moral carries with it serious conclusions, and of the utmost importance in these days. The Temporal Power of the Pope is a cause with which God and Religion are identified. That, consequently, there is only one right attitude for a Catholic with respect to it, namely, absolute detestation and abhorrence of any state of things which deprives the Pope of it. For to uphold in any way such a state of things, is to place one's self in opposition to God's own cause, in other words, to oppose God Himself. To be indifferent about it is hardly better; compromise is treachery. Our Lord Himself said: "He that is not with me is against Me." (Matthew xii.) There is no middle camp; not to be under Christ's standard is to be under Lucifer's. This is the whole meaning of the *"Non possumus"* attitude. It is not a question of politics, but one of Religion.

Giulio did not receive grace to shed his blood for politics, but to die for his Church.

My object in adding the following chapters to this interesting little biography is not only to give publicity to the events therein described, but also, and more especially, to make them the occasion, if possible, of a far wider circulation of the book than it at present enjoys; to make Giulio more universally known, and to place as many Catholics as possible within reach of that irresistible attraction which he continues to exercise, even though no longer on this earth, on all who make his acquaintance.

C. R. L.

ROME, *June, 1894.*

CHAPTER I.

The burial of Giulio's heart in the battle-field of Mentana in 1869—The Monument erected over it—Its destruction by the Garibaldians in 1870—Story of the saving of the heart and its transmission to England.

IN order that the reader may fully appreciate the interest of the recent events, which have brought about the present revival of Giulio's memory, I propose to start my work of publishing them by referring to certain interesting facts of the time immediately following his death, which, being subsequent to the first publication of the Biography, were not included in it.

It will appear from the Biography (pp. 61, 62,) that Giulio's body was buried in the cemetery of Monte Rotondo, together with others slain in the battle, and that it had not been in the ground many hours, when it was asked for by M. de Geneste, who arrived from Rome with authority to take it back there with him. Thereupon the body was at once exhumed by Colonel Woodward, Captain Shee and others, and handed over to M. de Geneste, who conveyed it to Rome as soon as possible. The events that followed its arrival at M. de Geneste's house, where it was embalmed and laid out for three days; its removal to the English College, where the last funeral rites were celebrated, and its ultimate interment in the Campo Verano, have been sufficiently described in the Biography.

In the process of embalming the body, the heart and other organs were removed. M. de Geneste kept the heart in his possession until he had an opportunity of handing it over to Mr. Watts-Russell (Giulio's father). It is not quite clear when this opportunity presented itself. Mr. Watts-Russell probably received it when he, together with his daughter, Ellen, came to Rome, a fortnight after Giulio's death, on which occasion took place the touching ceremony in the Campo Verano, described in the Biography (p. 9).

It is, however, quite certain that a year and a half later, namely, in April 1869, Giulio's father, having been ordained priest four months previously, accompanied by his son Wilfrid, arrived at Mentana, bearing with him the heart, which had been enclosed in a zinc case, and with considerable ceremony buried it in the battlefield, in the precise spot where the young hero fell. A little marble monument, consisting of a column about 3 feet high, surmounted by a marble cross (probably the Mentana cross), the whole enclosed by chains attached to four small colonnettes, was erected over it to mark the place. On the column was an appropriate inscription in Italian, composed, I believe, by the Rev. V. Cardella, S.J., recording in simple and concise terms the character of the young soldier's death, his age, and the fact that he was the youngest of the slain.

The story of this interesting and, indeed, touching little ceremony is told by the Rev. Giuseppe Franco, S.J., in his history of the campaign of 1867, entitled—*I Crociati di San Pietro* (Vol. III. pp. 524-5). He was himself present at it, and from his account it must have been a very impressive scene. The following is an extract, translated into English, of his description of the ceremony. "In the meanwhile the population of Mentana were being attracted to the spot, including several Zouaves of the neighbouring garrison. The workmen had dug up the earth; nothing remained but to perform the ceremony. Several priests were present; but the honour of officiating fell to an elderly man—a newly ordained priest. It was Giulio's father. Wilfrid, brother and fellow-soldier of Giulio, Mr. Vansittart, lately come to take the place of his deceased friend, and all of us pressed our lips to the metal case that enclosed the innocent and generous heart of the child crusader, and then it was deposited in the place prepared for it. Those affectionate kisses, those brotherly hands engaged in their office of piety and love, the right hand of the father, recently consecrated with the chrismatic oil, stretched out without trembling or hesitation over the remains of a beloved son, will never be effaced from our memory. We turned away feeling we had committed to the earth the relic of a martyr."

The monument erected over Giulio's heart in the battlefield of Mentana, was not solitary. I understand there were others raised there by relatives of the slain. Nevertheless, I have only certain knowledge of two others, namely, the one to Sergeant Rialan, occupying a site only a few yards distant from Giulio's, and the handsome marble column, raised to the memory of Captain de Veaux by his fellow soldiers in the Chapel of the Romitorio, close to which he fell.

These monuments, however, did not remain long to commemorate the valour of the soldiers thus honoured. A year and a half after the burial of Giulio's heart in the battlefield, took place those terrible events which all worthy sons of the Church still lament. In the sacrilegious attempt to crush the Church, its enemies, elated by their temporary apparent success, vented all their fury upon objects animate and inanimate that reminded them of former failures in a similar enterprise. Zouaves and their monuments were among the foremost of such objects; hence the abominable scenes enacted in Rome, immediately after it was seized in 1870; hence the wanton outrageous destruction of the Zouave monuments on the battlefield of Mentana in November of that year, when the Garibaldians assembled there for the first time to commemorate their defeat of 1867.

I believe it was generally thought at the time that Giulio's monument had been broken to pieces by the Garibaldians. At any rate, such seemed to be the prevalent opinion early this year among those who had any recollection of the events above described. It was in the month of February last, when paying a visit to Mentana, that I had the good fortune to discover that such was not the case, and was able to testify with absolute certainty to the existence, in a place of concealment, of the most important part of it, namely, the column on which the inscription was written. I also became possessed of certain letters, found to be in the keeping of a resident of Mentana, affording evidence which, in great measure, justifies the statements I am now about to make.

Before, however, relating the circumstances which led to the happy discovery of Giulio's monument (which I reserve to the next chapter), it behoves me to tell my readers what became of the heart buried under it, how it was saved from profanation. That I am now in a position to tell the somewhat romantic story of its rescue with accuracy, is owing, partly to the letters above mentioned, partly to information kindly afforded me by a surviving sister of Giulio (a religious in the Carmelite Convent of Darlington), but principally to the verbal and written testimonies of Signor Filippo Santucci and Signor Dottore Vespignani, both of Mentana, the former of whom I shall presently have to introduce to my readers more formally; the latter, the resident doctor of the town, who, having been to some extent concerned in the events to be described, has been able to supply me with much valuable information. From all these sources I have been able to put together the following narrative.

On the 3rd of November, 1870, took place at Mentana the first Garibaldian celebration of the battle of 1867. Among the crowd assembled there to take part in it, was a certain person, who seems to have had no object for being there at all, but to find Signor Dottore Vespignani and place a letter in his hands. This letter had no address on it, absolute secrecy regarding it being evidently of importance. A favourable opportunity presenting itself, this individual accosted the Doctor and delivered the letter into his hands, making no other remark but that he was commissioned to do so. The Doctor, rather surprised, took the letter, but before he could ask any questions the bearer had disappeared among the crowd, nor did the Doctor ever set eyes on him again.

The letter proved to be from the Rev. V. Cardella, S.J., Rector of the Community of Jesuits, forming the staff of the *Civiltà Cattolica*, at that time resident in the Piazza Scossa Cavalli, Rome.

The letter was worded more or less as follows:—"Mindful of your courteous hospitality last year, on the day of the ceremony in honour of Giulio Watts-Russell, I make bold to ask you to interest yourself in regard to the precious relic of the deceased, who was so dear to me, and have it placed out of reach of profanation. It is already known here that the monument has been knocked down and broken to pieces, and I cannot but fear that the few mortal remains of poor Giulio, buried underneath it, may be outraged in some similar manner. I beg you to do all in your power to rescue them, and God will reward you."

It appears that, after the ceremony of the burial of Giulio's heart in the previous year, Dottore Vespignani invited the Rev. M. Watts-Russell (Giulio's father), his son, Wilfrid, Fathers Cardella and Franco, S.J., to take some rest and refreshment in his house, before starting on their return journey to Rome. The company also included Signor Pietro Santucci, the Mayor of the town,[10] who had assisted at the ceremony. Father Cardella, therefore, took occasion from this act of hospitality to address the above letter to Dottore Vespignani, with whom he would otherwise have had no acquaintance whatever.

Dottore Vespignani determined that his best course was to hand the letter over to Signor Pietro Santucci, who, though no longer Mayor of Mentana, in consequence of the recent Piedmontese occupation, retained great influence among the townspeople. That this gentleman lost no time in carrying out the wishes expressed in the letter, may be gathered from the fact that he was able, the following morning, to inform the Doctor that Giulio's heart had been secretly exhumed the preceding night, by a man named Vincenzo Polognini, assisted by another, and was now safe and well cared for in his (Signor Santucci's) private house.

There remained now to discover a means of informing Father Cardella that the heart was safe, and that there was no further cause for anxiety. It was necessary also to establish communication with him, in order that a plan might be devised for the conveyance of the relic into proper hands. The times were abnormal; Mentana had no regular postal service, and, on the other hand, it would have been a great imprudence to send a letter, directed to a Jesuit, by any ordinary messenger. It so happened, however, by a fortu-

---

10   The owner of the Vigna Santucci, the principal scene of the battle of Mentana.

nate coincidence, that the Doctor's brother, Signor Raffaele Vespignani, had to go to Rome on business just at that time, and he consented to be a means of communication between Signor Santucci and Father Cardella, thereby solving one—and a very important—difficulty. Before he started, the three met together to decide on a safe method of procedure, to be followed by Signor Vespignani. The result of the conference was the following plan:—Signor R. Vespignani, on reaching Rome, was to go to the Church of the Gesu and present himself at the first Confessional he found occupied by a Jesuit priest. He was to ask the Reverend Father to instruct Father Cardella that, if on the following day, at the same hour, he (Father Cardella) should be in this same confessional, he would hear, from a certain person, the issue of a matter of great interest to him. On Father Cardella being found at the appointed time in the said confessional, Signor Vespignani was to let him know that Giulio's heart had been saved, and was in safe keeping; and he was to instruct him to send, on a certain day, a trustworthy messenger, to receive the precious object and bring it to Rome. This messenger, on reaching the Chapel of the Romitorio, situated one mile from Mentana, would meet the man who was to deliver up the casket containing the heart. To avoid all possibility of deception, and to ensure the safe conveyance of the casket into honest hands, Father Cardella was, furthermore, to instruct the messenger to ask the person he would meet, how much further it was to Mentana, and to look for the reply that it was six kilomètres distant.

The plan, thus devised, was strictly adhered to. Father Cardella was found by Signor Vespignani in the confessional at the time indicated, and, on hearing the proposed arrangement, readily consented to it. He asked two young men of his acquaintance to undertake the commission, but, whether from fear or some other motive, they declined. A third, however, readily consented, and when Father Cardella told him that his duty was to bring him Giulio Russell's heart, the youth corrected him, saying, "You mean, of course, Giulio *Watts* Russell's heart." "How do you know that is the right name?" asked Father Cardella. "Oh," said the young man, "I once copied a prayer to Our Lady that Giulio used to say, and his name was on it."

A better proof of the honesty of this willing messenger could scarcely be required; and he started off, feeling, no doubt, he had a pleasant, but at the same time, a responsible task to fulfil. I have not been able to ascertain who he was; Dottore Vespignani asserts that he represented himself as the hall porter of the *Civiltà Cattolica* establishment, but did not give his name, which is much to be regretted, as it deserves warm mention in this memoir.

All passed in the manner arranged. The young man, on reaching the Romitorio Chapel, situated, as before stated, within a mile of Mentana, met a person who, in fact, was none other than Signor Pietro Santucci aforesaid, ex-Mayor of Mentana. On being asked by the youth how far it was to Mentana, he replied, "Six kilomètres," and the casket containing Giulio's heart was accordingly delivered into the messenger's hands. The young man speedily returned with it to Rome, and placed it safely in the hands of Father Cardella, who, we may suppose, received it with the utmost joy and relief.

Father Cardella retained possession of Giulio's heart until he found a favourable opportunity for transmitting it to England. Such an opportunity did not present itself, apparently, till four months had gone by. Monsignor Stonor tells me that he was asked to take it in the month of December, when he was going to England on business, but that he refused, feeling that he could not be responsible for its safety, considering the troubled state of the countries he had to pass through. It does not appear who did ultimately take it; but there exists written evidence to show that it was sent from Rome on March 10th, 1871, and that in due course it came into the possession of the Rev. M. Watts-Russell (Giulio's father), then, I believe, residing in Bath. Without much delay he forwarded the casket to his daughter Ellen, who had already taken the veil in the Carmelite Convent at Darlington, and it was placed under the statue of Our Lady in the Nuns' choir, where it still reposes.

The Rev. M. Watts-Russell wrote a letter of gratitude to Signor Pietro Santucci; and Father Cardella sent him, in token of appreciation of his noble conduct, a framed photograph of Giulio in Zouave gala dress. Several letters, also, were exchanged between them relative to these events, which I intend to notice in a subsequent chapter.

Pius IX., having been duly informed of all that had taken

place, sent, through Father Cardella, his blessing to the Rev. M. Watts-Russell and his family—a fitting conclusion to so remarkable a series of events.

CHAPTER II.

Discovery of Giulio's Monument at Mentana in February, 1894, and the circumstances that led to it—The Monument conveyed to the Church of St. Thomas of Canterbury, at the English College, Rome, and restored.

SIGNOR Pietro Santucci died in the year 1878, leaving his Mentana property divided between five sons. Of these, the eldest does not reside there. The other four still continue to live at Mentana, their names being Filippo, Giacomo, Domenico, and Laureto. They spend their time, I believe, working their respective portions of the land, and live together in the family residence, situated adjoining the parish Church of the town. As Signor Filippo is the only one who has had a part in the events to be described in this chapter, him alone do I introduce to my readers.

The revival of Giulio's memory, twenty-seven years after his death, dates back to January 31st of the present year, 1894. On this day my friend, Monsignor Merry del Val (Cam. Seg. Part. to His Holiness Leo XIII.), had occasion to visit

Signor Filippo Santucci at Mentana on business concerning a valuable collection of relics, existing in the private Chapel of the family residence. It appears that Monsignor Merry del Val failed to give sufficient notice of his coming, so that, on arriving at Mentana, he found that Signor Filippo was absent for the day in Rome. However, the other brothers were at home, and they showed him all objects of interest in their house, including the Chapel in which the relics were kept. On emerging from the Chapel into an adjoining chamber, Monsignor Merry del Val noticed a framed photograph hanging on the wall, which attracted his attention by reason of its representing a Pontifical Zouave in full gala uniform. Moreover he felt certain he had seen that portrait before. After wiping the dust off the glass to obtain a clearer view of the picture, he exclaimed: "Why! this is Julian Watts-Russell; where did you get this photograph from?" One of the brothers replied that it had belonged to their father, but did not offer any further explanation. Whereupon Monsignor Merry del Val, influenced by its somewhat neglected appearance, from which he inferred that it was not much valued by its present possessors, expressed a wish to become the owner of it, and hoped they would give it to him. The request was not granted at once by the brothers, who, perhaps, hesitated about the propriety of giving the photograph away in the absence of their elder brother. Monsignor Merry del Val, noticing their hesitation, concluded that they were not willing to part with it, and did not press his request. It was rather to his surprise, therefore, that the photograph was handed to him, wrapped in paper, as he was starting on his return drive to Rome.

He bore it triumphantly away and, a few days later, I saw it myself hanging in his sitting room in the Vatican.

Monsignor Merry del Val's story of his visit to Mentana reminded me that I had had for some time past, the intention of visiting that place, so interesting in its associations. My opportunity came a few days later, namely, February 5. On this day, I, accompanied by a friend, made a day's excursion to Mentana, proceeding by train to Monte Rotondo, and thence on foot the remainder of the distance. Mentana is about 2 miles from the railway station of Monte Rotondo, and is accessible by a good carriage road, commanding fine views of the valley of the Tiber and the mountains of the Sabine district. The town of Monte Rotondo, which the road skirts, is finely situated on high ground. There is nothing of any great interest to be seen there excepting, perhaps, the palace, which formerly belonged to the Orsini family; but it was the scene of splendid fighting by Pontifical and French soldiers in the campaign of 1867.

We reached Mentana at about midday, and during the preparation of our dinner at the Café Picucci, we took a walk round the Vigna Santucci, which, as before stated, was the principal scene of the battle of 1867. The Vigna is situated on rising ground, overlooking the town, and its strength from a military point of view must be evident to any observer. Without pretending to any knowledge in the art of warfare, I think I may safely assert, that, owing to the position of the town, no successful attack could be made on it except from the Vigna Santucci; and this because the Vigna slopes directly into the heart of the town, whereas the heights on the opposite side descend into a narrow ravine, from which an ascent has to be made to gain the town. That the battle of 1867 was won by the Pontifical soldiers, was largely, if not entirely, owing to their driving the Garibaldians off this ground, and, assisted by the French, ultimately retaining possession of it. Had they been unsuccessful in this, Mentana would not have been surrendered, and Rome might have been taken three years sooner than it was.

The glorious view commanded from the summit of the Vigna quite repays the visitor for the fatigue of the ascent. But marks of the battle are scarcely to be found, nothing more, in fact, than a few shot marks on the gate, a half demolished monument inviting the passer-by to pray for the repose of the souls of the Zouaves who fell in the fight, and a monstrous erection, raised by the Italian Government to commemorate the valour of those, on whom they forced the inglorious enterprise of fighting against the Church, and whom they are pleased to number among the country's heroes. This Garibaldian monument, however, must not be passed by unnoticed by an English son of the Church, for it marks the place where Giulio fell, shot through the brain.[11]

Whilst we were exploring the ground, we met a gentlemanly looking person, who courteously addressed us, and

---

11   *It will be well here to comment on a statement made in the Biography (p. 54), to the effect that Giulio was shot from a window. It seems by no means evident that it was so. Captain Shee thinks it impossible; for Giulio's face was much burnt by the flame of the discharge, which would show that he was at very close quarters with his adversary. No such effect could have been produced by a gun fired from any of the windows looking on to the approach from the Vigna. There seems to be some mystery concerning the manner in which Giulio met his death.

with whom we entered into conversation, hoping he would show us points of interest in connection with the battle. Although not able to tell us much more than we already knew, he made himself very agreeable, and was ready to offer us any assistance we might require. In course of conversation he asked me whether I was acquainted with Monsignor Merry del Val, and on my replying in the affirmative, referred to his visit to Mentana a few days previous. He then asked me whether I could conveniently convey him a message. I expressed my readiness to do so, and begged to know from whom I was to carry it. "My name," he said, "is Signor Filippo Santucci." "Oh," said I, rather taken back, "are you the owner of the Vigna Santucci?"

"I own a portion of it," he replied; "it was my father who owned it at the time of the battle. He died about seventeen years ago, and the estate was divided among all the sons. The part where the battle took place belongs to my eldest brother, who does not live here."

"Well," I said, "I am very pleased to have made your acquaintance, and only too glad to carry your message to Monsignor Merry del Val, if you will kindly tell me what I am to say to him."

"It is this," he said; "Monsignor Merry del Val came here a few days ago to see me on a matter of business. Unfortunately, not knowing he was coming, I was absent all that day. My brother, however, received him in our house, and he happened to find there a photograph which I valued highly. He asked my brothers to let him have it, and they gave it to him. I was most vexed when, on my return, I found it had been given away. Had I been at home, I would have refused to part with it; I would willingly have lent it to him for a short time, in order that he might have a reproduction made, but I would not have made him a present of it."

"You refer," said I, "to the photograph of Giulio Watts Russell?"

"Yes," he replied, "Russell was the name of the youth whose portrait it was. I will tell you how it came into my father's possession."

He then told me the story of the burial of Giulio's heart in the battle-field, the monument over it, and the Garibaldian outrage, followed by the saving of the heart, very much as I have told it in Chapter I., only less fully. It was the first time I had heard it, and, as may be supposed, both my friend and I were deeply interested. On Signor Santucci reaching the end of his narrative, I begged to know how I could assist him. "Well, sir," he replied, "I would esteem it as a great favour if you would kindly ask Monsignore to have the photograph reproduced and send me a copy." I readily promised to do so, and, in fact, undertook to have it reproduced myself. This ended our interview, and he bade us both farewell, after cordially thanking me. A few minutes later, my friend and I were on our way back to Rome, which we reached shortly after dark.

The interest aroused in me by Signor Santucci's story in no way declined, and so, within two days of my return from Mentana, I was on my way to the Vatican to obtain the photograph from Monsignor Merry del Val. On my submitting to him Signor Santucci's request, he kindly lent me the portrait for the purpose of reproduction, and I handed it over to the Rev. Thomas Dunn, at that time a co-resident of mine in Rome, renowned for his skill in photography. He succeeded in producing two excellent negatives from the original—a large and a small size. Numerous copies were at once printed off them, the applications for them being many, as soon as the success of the reproduction became known. A good specimen was set aside for Signor Santucci, and framed similarly to the original. It was ready by February 15th, on which day I paid a second visit to Mentana to present it to him. Father Dunn accompanied me on this occasion, in order to photograph the battlefield and points of interest round about it.

It was on this day that Giulio's monument was so happily discovered. Whether or no the reproduced copy of the photograph had the effect of loosening Signor Santucci's tongue, I cannot say. But certain it is that after I had given it to him, he afforded us the surprising information that a portion of the monument still existed. I was very much taken back by this news, for from Signor Santucci's former account of the events concerning the saving of the heart, I had been led to suppose that the monument had been destroyed, like the other monuments in the battlefield, all of which were ultimately broken to pieces, no vestige of them remaining. That Signor Santucci intended to convey this impression, there seems but little doubt; for it was evidently his purpose to prevent the existence of the monument being made known among the Mentana people.

On my asking where the monument was, he replied that it was down in the cellar underneath the Café Picucci (before mentioned). To leave Mentana without seeing it was not to be thought of, so I asked permission to go down and look at it. The proprietor consenting, and lights having been obtained, we all went down to examine this interesting object. Arrived at the bottom of the flight of steps, we found ourselves in a place to which the term "cellar" could not strictly be applied; for although it was under the Café, it was not underground, there being an exit from it into the fields on the side of the hill, on which the town is built. It was apparently used for stacking wood, housing poultry, and perhaps, other farm yard animals. Standing in the middle of this so-called cellar was a marble column about 3 ft. high, bearing on it the following inscription:—

QUI MORI
PUGNANDO PRO SEDE PETRI
GIULIO WATTS RUSSELL
ZOUAVO PONTIFICIO
GIOVANETTO INGLESE
D'ANNI 17 E 10 MESI
IL PIU GIOVANE
CADUTO NEL CAMPO DELLA VITTORIA
E IL PIU D'APPRESSO A MENTANA
LA SUA VITA
COMPENDIASI NEL SUO MOTTO

ANIMA MIA, ANIMA MIA
AMA DIO E TIRA VIA.[12]

Nothing could be more interesting at this moment than the discovery of Giulio's monument, following, as it did, almost immediately on my hearing, for the first time, the story of its supposed destruction and the saving of the heart. Instead of having been broken to pieces, it had somehow escaped the ultimate fate of the other monuments, and had been lying concealed for over 23 years, unthought of and practically out of reach of those who would be most interested in knowing of its existence.

My ideas being for the moment somewhat confused, at the sight of this column, to which such moving associations were attached, it was impossible to form a clear opinion on the spot as to the right course to follow with regard to it. One thing, however, was at once evident, namely, the impropriety of leaving it in this dirty cellar. Signor Santucci acknowledged the unfitness of the place, but accounted for the monument being left there by the fact of it having been necessary in former times to keep it out of sight, to secure it from injury; and this cellar was as good a hiding-place for it as could be found. I remarked that a more worthy locality ought at once to be found for it; a remark which had a good effect, for on the following day Signor Santucci removed it to his own house in the Vigna. It did not remain there long, as will presently appear.

---

12   These last lines are inscribed on the back of the column.

It will not be without interest to note here, that Father Dunn and I came upon another Zouave monument on this day, in the Chapel of the Romitorio, about a mile from Mentana, on the high road to Rome. This chapel was one of the objects to be photographed, for it may be said to mark the place where the battle commenced. In those days, I am told, the chapel was intact, and served on Sundays for the benefit of the peasantry. Now it is a ruin and desecrated by Garibaldian profanations. The outer wall, facing the road, is covered with names, chiefly of Pontifical soldiers who have since visited the scene of the conflict. As it stands it is a monument of their bravery, and a witness of the hatred of religion animating those, or some of those, who were sent to wrest from the Holy See its remaining temporal possessions. But it is not only a monument of the battle in general, it bears also very particular reference to Giulio; for it was the place of rendez-vous between Signor Pietro Santucci and the messenger sent by Father Cardella to bring Giulio's heart to Rome, at the time of its rescue.

Entering this ruined chapel and descending the broken steps that led to a subterranean oratory, Father Dunn and I found a large white marble column lying deeply imbedded in the débris at the foot of the steps. As that side of it was uppermost on which was written a French inscription, we were able, after removing some of the earth, to identify it as the monument raised to Captain De Veaux by his fellow soldiers, already referred to in Chapter I. Captain de Veaux was one of the very first to fall in the battle of Mentana; he was shot through the heart within a few yards of the chapel.

When Father Dunn and I took leave of Signor Santucci to return to Rome, he told us that he would be coming to Rome in a few days; and would bring with him, for my inspection, certain letters he had in his possession, bearing on the events concerning the saving of Giulio's heart and the destruction of the monument. He fulfilled this promise on February 19th. The letters he brought proved to be of considerable interest and importance, and it is from them that I derive my authority for many of the statements I have made and am about to make. There were four letters altogether, of which three were from the Rev. V. Cardella, S.J., to Signor Pietro Santucci, and one from the Rev. M. Watts-Russell (Giulio's father) to the same, thanking him in warm terms for having rescued his son's heart from profanation. Signor Filippo Santucci subsequently brought me copies of his father's replies to these letters, also containing interesting matter. As I intend publishing these and several other letters regarding Giulio, that have come into my possession, in a subsequent chapter, I make no further reference to them at present.

Two days prior to Signor Santucci's arrival in Rome with the first four letters, I had decided to act on a suggestion, proposed by one or two persons, namely, that Giulio's monument should be brought to the English College in Rome, and placed in the Church there. Accordingly I obtained the consent of Monsignor Giles, Rector of the College, to negociate with Signor Santucci to that end; the consent being given on the understanding that all expenses incurred should be met by subscription. When, therefore, Signor Santucci paid me his visit, I took the opportunity of approaching him on this subject, and asked him to state on what terms he would consent to part with the monument. I expected he would make considerable objection to the proposal of bringing it to Rome, or, at least, would make it a question of money. Much to my surprise, he agreed to it most willingly, and absolutely refused to accept anything for it. He said he considered it his duty to let me have it under the circumstances, and, bearing in mind the wishes of his father regarding it, he would not place any impediment in the way of our restoring it in the English College Church, which he regarded as a most fitting place for it. I might, therefore, have it when I liked, and, moreover, he would be pleased to lend me his assistance in the matter of its transport.

This generosity and right feeling on the part of Signor Santucci was, indeed, most gratifying. I cordially thanked him, and readily accepted the offer of his assistance. Before he returned to Mentana, it was arranged that the monument should be brought to Rome as soon as possible.

Within a week from Signor Santucci's visit, I received news from him, that he had arranged with a carter for the conveyance of the column on the following day, February 23rd. Accordingly, on that morning, I went out to Mentana to assist in the work in whatever way might be required, and accompany the monument to Rome. At Signor Santucci's kind invitation, I dined with him in his house on the Vigna, after which he and I started for Rome in a vehicle of somewhat rough build, drawn by a horse of impaired constitution; the best, however, that the town could afford us. The carter had started with the monument about two hours before us, and we expected to overtake him about 5 miles short of the city. As a matter of fact, we came up with him just after passing over the Nomentana bridge, which crosses the river Anio, two miles from the Porta Pia. A few yards further we were met by the Very Rev. J. Prior, D.D., Vice-Rector of the English College, who joined us in our fly. The monument was passed through the custom house without difficulty, and Rome was reached at 5 o'clock. Before 6 o'clock both the monument and ourselves had arrived at the English College, and the interesting journey was at an end.

The restoration of the monument was taken in hand without delay. A stone-cutter was at once called in, to design a suitable marble pedestal for the column, and within two days of its arrival at the College, had received orders to execute the work. The order for the restoration of the cross was, however, delayed a short time, pending enquiries as to the form and material of the original cross; regarding which there was considerable doubt at first, for Signor Santucci himself never saw the monument on its first site on the battlefield, and there was no one to be found in Rome who remembered it. The doubt was ultimately solved by the testimony of Dottore Vespignani, whose name appears in the last chapter in connection with the saving of Giulio's heart. At the time of the discovery of the monument, I knew nothing of the part this gentleman had taken in the transaction, and thus never thought of referring to him, until Signor Santucci now told me that there still resided at Mentana the doctor who was present at the ceremony of the burial of the heart in 1869, and could doubtless give all information I was in search of regarding the cross. On applying to him, I was fortunate in obtaining of him a sufficiently detailed description of the original cross, to enable me to decide how it should be restored. From his saying it was a Greek cross of marble, with inscriptions on the arms, little doubt could exist but that it was a marble cross of the design of the Mentana medal (*i.e.*, the decoration given by Pius IX. to the soldiers who had taken part in the campaign). Accordingly the stone-cutter was instructed to make a marble cross after this design, with all the embossed work of the medal carved *in relievo*.

The order for this cross was not given until it was found that the appeal for subscriptions was being generously responded to. Indeed, one of the most gratifying features of the revival of Giulio's memory this year has been the sympathy shown by the English colony in Rome with all the work done to venerate him. The subscription list was opened on February 26th. In two days I had £6 at my disposal, which sum had risen to £20 by the end of March. This speaks for itself; Giulio had not been forgotten; his noble and saintly character, his heroic death, was still impressed on the minds of those who knew him in life, and appealed no less to those whose acquaintance with him was only from history. But not only was money forthcoming from English residents in Rome. I have had, also, to acknowledge generous offerings from

England, Germany, and even New York. Most satisfactory, above all, has been the warm encouragement accorded me by the surviving brother and sister of Giulio, and I have to thank them both for much valuable information.

The restoration of the monument was completed in about two months' time. The pedestal was finished on April 4th, and the cross, the carving on which had been executed by a sculptor specially called in for the purpose, was fixed in its place about a fortnight later. The monument, as it now stands in the left aisle of the English College Church, may be described as follows: The column found at Mentana stands on a pedestal of white marble nearly 1ft. in height and 1ft. 7in. square, on the top of which is a circular moulding about six inches high, cut out hollow, to allow of the column passing through it, and resting on the pedestal. The cross surmounting the column is an exact reproduction of the Mentana medal in white marble, measuring 1ft. in breadth, 1ft. 2in. in height, and about 1in. in thickness. The whole monument, from the floor to the top of the cross, stands about 5ft. 2in. in height. The letters of the original inscription are varnished black to make them easily readable. On the pedestal the following has been inscribed in red letters:—

THIS MONUMENT
ERECTED AT MENTANA IN 1869
OUTRAGED AND THROWN DOWN IN 1870
BROUGHT TO THIS CHURCH AND RESTORED IN 1894

COMMEMORATES THE FAITH AND COURAGE OF[13]
JULIAN WATTS RUSSELL
WHO SHED HIS BLOOD FOR THE HOLY SEE
NOVEMBER 3, 1867.

Thus is Giulio's monument re-dedicated, after 23 years' concealment, to its office of publicly proclaiming his heroic death in defence of the rights of the Church.

The discovery and restoration of this monument led to other events, not less interesting, to the recording of which the following chapters are devoted.

Julian Watts-Russell's monument, taken in 1894.

---

13   These words, "Faith and Courage," occur on the face of the Mentana medal—*"Fidei et Virtuti."*

Twenty-Seven Years Later — 1895

Julian Watts-Russell's monument, taken in 2024. Notice how the Mentan model at the top is facing the reverse direction 130 years later. Perhaps a seminarian accidently broke it at some point and repaired it wrong.

CHAPTER III.

Giulio's grave in the Campo Verano—Exhumation and re-interment of his remains—Repair of the grave.

TO repair Giulio's grave and make it as far as possible worthy of him, entered into my purpose the day I paid my first visit to it, some time in March. In truth, I was shocked by its neglected and bare appearance. A simple headstone was the only indication that the precious remains of the young hero reposed underneath; and this headstone was decidedly on the road to disintegration. The cross surmounting it was loose in its socket and could be removed at will; the marble work immediately underneath it was detached from the rest of the stone, and only required a push for it to fall to the ground. The rest of the monument was by no means secure, and the inscription was becoming unreadable. To leave the grave in this state, when an opportunity was afforded of repairing it, would have been to show a want of respect to Giulio's memory, for which the restoration of his Mentana monument in the English College, would hardly have compensated.

Twenty-Seven Years Later — 1895

As soon as it became generally known that some work of repair at the grave was contemplated, two or three important suggestions were made with regard to the remains. For instance, one evening, in conversation with the Rev. T. Armellini, S.J., who had been Giulio's confessor in Rome, on my referring to the wretched state of the grave, I was somewhat taken back by his expressing an opinion that the remains should be transferred to the English College Church. I objected that the authorities would hardly permit such a thing, and even if they did it would be necessary to obtain the consent of the family, which I doubted would be given. He replied that as far as the law was concerned, it could be done; for it was allowed to bring a body to a city church ten years after its first burial. This statement was subsequently corroborated by others, and it seemed, for a time, that such a course could be adopted without difficulty. Another suggestion made was that the remains should be sent to Ushaw College—Giulio's "Alma Mater,"—on condition that the College should bear the expense of the transport; a proposition, which at first commended itself to my mind, as I knew well Giulio's body would receive honour and respect there, which would never be shown it in the Roman cemetery.

Thus there were three alternatives proposed with regard to the body:—(1) Removing it to England; (2) Removing it to the English College Church in Rome; (3) Leaving it in its original resting place, in the Campo Verano, and restoring the tomb.

The decision as to which of these courses should be

adopted, obviously rested with the Rev. M. Watts-Russell (Giulio's surviving brother), whose authority was, of course, necessary for carrying out any alterations with regard to his brother's grave. His reply to the letter I wrote to him on the matter, was to the effect that of all courses proposed, the removal of the body to the English College met most with his approval. He preferred that to doing up the grave.

On receipt of this letter, I at once sought the best means of carrying out the wishes expressed in it. Through the kindness of the Very Rev. W. Whitmee, S.M., Rector of the Church of San Silvestro in Capite, I obtained an introduction to Signor Cavaliere Trucchi, Chief Inspector of the Cemetery at the Campo Verano, whose assistance, no matter what course was adopted, was indispensable. On my submitting to him the plan of moving the body to the English College, he said it was quite impossible; and in reference to the statement made that the law permitted bodies to be brought to the churches after a lapse of ten years, he informed me that it was no longer so. The law now strictly forbade any corpse from re-entering the city, no matter how long a time had passed since death, and there was no exception admitted under any circumstances. But with regard to the other alternatives, he said that both of them could easily be carried out, and kindly offered me every possible assistance in the matter.

The result of this interview was reported to the Rev. M. Watts-Russell, and his instructions asked for. Pending their arrival, I made an appointment with Signor Trucchi to visit the grave with me, in order to obtain an estimate of the probable cost of the work I proposed to have done, if it were decided to restore the tomb. We met at the cemetery with this object on May 5th. He carefully examined the headstone and the ground in front of it, and, on my describing my plan of improvement, told me I must be prepared to spend about £16,—a sum which, at first, rather alarmed me, for at the moment I only had between £6 and £7 at my disposal for the work, and it seemed doubtful that I could raise a further £10 by subscription. Father Watts-Russell's letter arrived in a few days, and determined finally what was to be done. Giulio's body was to remain in its present resting place, since it could not be removed to the English College. The writer was convinced that Giulio himself would prefer his remains to continue to rest in Rome, if his wishes could be consulted.

I heartily agreed with this decision. There were, no doubt, arguments in favour of having the body conveyed to England, and especially to Ushaw; but on the other hand there was evident fitness and congruity in their not being removed from the vicinity of the "*cryptae martyrum,*" nor from the territory in defence of which the young soldier gave up his life. Add to these reasons the close proximity of his grave to that of the Sovereign, whose soldier he was, and to that of the General in command of the army to which he belonged, and it will be generally conceded that the reasons for leaving the body in the grave first prepared for it, outweighed those in support of its removal.

But what was most important about Father Watts-Russell's letter was, that he gave me in it full authority to open the coffin and examine the condition of the remains. I had been moved to ask for this, principally for the following reason. It will be seen from the Biography (page 9), that Giulio's coffin was opened, and his body exposed to view twenty days after death, for the consolation of his father, sister and brother, and that it was found not only incorrupt, but also extraordinarily flexible in every limb. Now this was either supernatural or not. If it was supernatural, then a possibility existed of there being a continuance of Divine interference with the ordinary laws at the present time. That there should have been no sign of decomposition would have been, by itself, nothing wonderful, seeing that the body had been embalmed; but the flexibility of all the limbs was justly regarded as most remarkable. I have been told that embalming a body has not the effect of preventing it from stiffening; and that flexibility of limb in a preserved body is regarded as a supernatural sign.

For these and other reasons, there was a prevalent opinion in Rome, among those interested in Giulio, that his body might still be incorrupt; and it seemed right, therefore, to place the matter, once and for all, beyond all doubt. In the event of the body being found still perfect, it clearly ought to be known and examined into, with a view to deciding how far it was a natural or supernatural state of things; and if it had decomposed like all other bodies, all possibility of the contrary being asserted, or hinted at, should be done away with.

It was with much satisfaction, therefore, that I obtained

permission to open Giulio's grave. It is only just to say, that the leave was granted solely through the kindness and courtesy of Signor Cavaliere Trucchi, who, on my receiving the necessary authority from Father Watts-Russell, undertook to arrange the matter without delay. His promptitude and readiness to oblige may be judged from the fact, that on the same day as Father Watts-Russell's letter reached me, namely, May 12th, the exhumation was fixed for the 16th at 6 a.m.

Although Signor Trucchi had warned me that the work of opening the grave was to be done quite privately, and that, strictly speaking, he was entitled to exclude every one, without exception, from the cemetery whilst it was going on, he nevertheless consented to my being present, accompanied by seven other persons. The following were, therefore, invited to attend: Monsignor Merry del Val (Cam. Seg. Part. to His Holiness Leo XIII., and formerly of Ushaw College); the Rev. T. Armellini, S.J. (Giulio's confessor in Rome); Monsignor G. de Stacpoole (Domestic Prelate to His Holiness Leo XIII.); the Very Rev. J. Prior (Vice-Rector of the English College); the Rev. A. Hinsley (formerly an Ushaw student); Dr. Eyre (of the Royal College of Physicians, present in case medical testimony should be required); Count de Raymond (whose mother, the Countess de Raymond, was intimate with, and related to Giulio, as seen from the Biography).

On the morning of May 16th, therefore, the above-mentioned persons and I assembled at the Campo Verano at 6 o'clock, to do honour to Giulio's remains. We were received at the entrance to the cemetery by Signor Cavaliere Trucchi, who had preceded us to make preliminary arrangements, and without delay we proceeded to the grave. The tombstone had already been removed, and some of the earth put aside two days previous, so that but little work was now needed to open the grave entirely. The men, under the direction of Signor Trucchi, commenced to work at about 6-15. Some more of the earth having been removed, it was found that the body was resting in a vault, and not buried in contact with the earth—a form of burial usually adopted in Rome in cases of well-to-do persons. Thus the men had nothing now to do but to break up the cement uniting the stones that closed the vault, and remove the stones themselves.

It was soon evident that the vault had been very imperfectly closed in the first instance, and the stones badly fitted together. Consequently, on these stones being with some difficulty raised, and the interior of the vault brought to view, traces of rain having penetrated into it were clearly noticeable. A zinc coffin, very much broken, was the first object that met our eyes, and all round it the decayed remains of the wooden coffin that had originally enclosed the zinc one. The damaged state of the zinc coffin was clearly attributable to the entrance of water, the principal indication of this being that the lid was bent inwards to such a degree, as to cause it to be torn away from the sides. Through the rents thus formed it was clear that the moisture must have found easy entrance into the interior of the coffin. The full extent of the damage came to light, on the coffin being brought to the surface, and ripped open. There was then no further question of incorruption, natural or supernatural. The rain had brought about general decomposition of everything, and had completely rotted the metal. Even the bones of the skeleton, which ought to have been sound, were very much injured, and the skull was entirely broken away on one side—possibly the effect of the fatal shot.

It being clear that the remains could not be left in this state, and as there was no time available for discussion as to what should be done, it seemed best to acquiesce at once in the proposal, made by Signor Trucchi, that the bones of the skeleton should be transferred to a new zinc casket. And, in fact, from many points of view, this was perhaps the best course to adopt. For, first, as the bones had to be removed from the original coffin, it would have been impossible, owing to the state they were in, to arrange them again at full length, and, for this reason alone a casket was preferable to a full-sized coffin. Secondly, the bones enclosed in a casket would be better preserved from the influence of damp, there being less danger of a small casket breaking than a full-sized coffin. Thirdly, in the event of the remains being sent to England at some future date, it would be easier to send them in a casket than in an ordinary coffin.

The transferring of the bones was, therefore, consented to. But before any change was made, I carefully examined the coffin to see whether the paper on which had been copied the Protestation of Fidelity to our Blessed Lady, from Giulio's manuscript prayer-book, was anywhere to be found. I refer to the prayer spoken of in the Biography (pages 87-8), and it will be remembered that a copy of it, written by Giulio's sister, was placed in the coffin by his father, the first time it was opened some twenty days after death. (See Biography, page 9). My search, however, proved fruitless. The paper had shared in the general corruption, as might have been expected. The only objects we found in the coffin, and took away with us, were seven shirt buttons belonging to the shirt that clothed the body at the time of burial.

A zinc casket being obtainable at once, the removal of the skeleton was quickly done. The casket was then soldered up, and on to the side of it was affixed the plate, which had been on the original wooden coffin, bearing the following inscription:—

JULIAN WATTS RUSSELL
PONTIFICAL ZOUAVE, 2nd COMP., 1st BAT.
DIED AT MENTANA, 3rd NOVEMBER, 1867.
REQUIESCAT IN PACE.

Before the remains were replaced in the vault, which had now been swept thoroughly clean, at our request, Signor Trucchi sent over to the church of San Lorenzo to ask a Capuchin Father to come and perform such religious function as should be thought proper. The Rev. Father read a portion of the burial service and blessed the new casket, which was then re-interred. The whole ceremony finished with the closing of the vault, two hours after the work of exhumation had begun.

Although all those who were present at the ceremony

expressed themselves as quite satisfied with what had been done, I confess I was not, at first; and this, owing to the complete destruction of the above-mentioned prayer, which, in so far as it was involved in the old coffin being burnt up, I was in some way responsible for. Reasonably or unreasonably, I was considerably disturbed in mind about it, and felt guilty, in some measure, of violating Giulio's wish that the prayer should be buried with him, a wish that had been so carefully respected by his father and sister. These feelings did not diminish as time went on; and so, when a few days later I paid a visit to Signor Trucchi to thank him for his kindness in the matter of the exhumation of the body, I was led to tell him the whole story regarding this prayer, and to express the regret I felt at not having had an opportunity of replacing it. To my surprise, without any hesitation, he spontaneously offered to allow me to open the casket again for the purpose of replacing the prayer, agreeing at the same time in the propriety of doing so. I readily accepted his offer, and thanked him most cordially for his renewed kindness.

The prayer was, at my request, written out by Giulio's sister, the Carmelite religious of Darlington, it being obviously fitting that it should be in her handwriting. I received it from her on May 25th, and on the following morning the vault was once more opened and the prayer placed in the casket, together with another paper, on which was drawn up a declaration, signed by all those who attended the exhumation ceremony of the 16th, setting forth the date of the translation of the remains to the casket, and the reason why it was done.

It is interesting to note that this was the fifth time that Giulio's remains had been exposed to view since his death. The dead remains of very few persons have commanded such interest as this.

My fears that sufficient money would not be forthcoming for repairing the grave suitably, proved to be groundless. Further generous subscriptions were received, and I was able to carry out my design for its improvement. The work, which was completed by the end of May, consisted in thoroughly re-facing and repairing the original headstone, with its cross, and re-erecting it on a new foundation. Every letter of the inscription also was re-filled with molten lead. The ground immediately in front of the headstone (under which repose the remains), was enclosed within coping stone work of white marble, into which were fitted six marble colonnettes, supporting a brass railing. The enclosed space was then filled with earth, and various kinds of flowers planted in it.

The cost of this work amounted to £17, and the result is eminently satisfactory. Giulio's grave is certainly more worthy of him now than it was before, and although simple and unpretending in design, it compares very favourably with the more elaborately carved monuments that surround it; many of which pretend unsuccessfully to being works of art. Arrangements have been made for its future maintenance, and it is hoped that there will always be found some, among English residents in Rome, who will take interest in it, and pay it an occasional visit.

My narrative will not be complete unless I submit to my

readers some of the written matter I have been fortunate in being able to collect regarding Giulio, consisting, chiefly, of letters written shortly after his death. As much interesting information is afforded by them, I propose to make them the subject of the two following chapters.

CHAPTER IV.

The Mentana Letters; also other Letters, recently found, written soon after Giulio's death.

IN Chapter II., I mentioned that Signor Filippo Santucci of Mentana, handed over to me certain letters, written to his father, bearing reference to the destruction of Giulio's monument, and the saving of his heart in 1870. He kindly lent me the originals for a short time, in order that I might take copies of them; and he, moreover, obliged me by copying his father's replies to these letters, for my use. As this correspondence throws some light on the events described in Chapter I., and also proves, in a great measure, the truth of the story therein told, I propose here to reproduce them. They were, of course, written in Italian, but for the benefit of those of my readers who are not acquainted with that language, I have translated them into equivalent English.

The first letter to be published is one written by the Rev. M. Watts-Russell (Giulio's father), thanking Signor Pietro Santucci for having rescued his son's heart.

Nov. 27th, 1870.
7, Queen's Parade, Bath.

Dear Sir,

I received, a few days ago, a letter from Father V. Cardella, conveying the joyful news that Signor Santucci has had the charity and courage to rescue from profanation a precious relic at Mentana, (viz., the heart of my dearest son, Julian).

Being a foreigner, I am not able to find words to express, as ought to be expressed, my sincere gratitude, and the deep emotion of my paternal heart. I can only, in my unworthy prayers, beg our Lord to reward Signor Santucci eternally for the love he has shown my son.

I remain, dear Sir,
Your most humble servant in Jesus Christ,
M. WATTS-RUSSELL.

This letter is of especial interest, as affording satisfactory evidence that it really is to Signor Pietro Santucci we owe the fact of Giulio's heart being now in safe keeping.

The following is a letter written by the Rev. V. Cardella, S.J. (Civiltà Cattolica, Rome), to Signor Pietro Santucci:—

Civiltà Cattolica,
Piazza Scossa Cavalli, No. 66.

Dear Sir,

I have delayed until now writing to thank you for what you have done, partly to avoid all possibility of compromising you, by directing a letter to you through the post, and partly because I wished to be able to thank you, also, in the name of Mr. Watts-Russell, to whom I wrote and told our benefactor's name. I enclose, with much pleasure, the letter which he himself has written in Italian.

I add, in token of my own gratitude, a photograph of Giulio, which I would wish you to keep, as a reminiscence of your good work. May our Lord reward you in this and in the next life.

Believe me,
Your grateful and humble servant,
V. CARDELLA, S.J.

Civiltà Cattolica, 1st Dec., 1870.

This letter was not sent off for over a month, and the following was added later on the same paper:—

Dear Sir,

For the reason already mentioned, I have put off sending this letter until to-day, the Feast of the Epiphany. But by this time no suspicions will be aroused by your receiving a letter and a parcel from Rome. Nevertheless, with regard to the parcel, in other words, the photograph, which I have had framed, I shall not send it now, but will wait until I receive instructions from you as to the best way of sending it. I am acquainted with someone who has connection with Mentana, namely, Signor Giomini, and I also know the Barbiellini family; but I would not risk sending it by them without your directions. Of course, no matter to whom it is consigned, there is no need to say what it is, or why it is sent. I beg you, therefore, to determine the means of sending you this token of my gratitude, and to say whether you wish me to keep it until a more favourable opportunity presents itself. But now will you kindly tell me, as much as possible in detail, what the Garibaldians have done to that monument. I have heard from the Barbiellini that the monument was smashed, not on the 3rd of November, as I thought, but as far back as September 20th. What has become of the column, and particularly of the cross? Do any of the pieces of the cross remain? But above all I am anxious to know how came about the breakage of the upper part of the leaden tube. It hardly seems possible that it could be a chance breakage, brought about by digging it up. Perhaps the Garibaldians broke it, and, moreover, have perhaps broken the interior earthenware vessel. I have had the breakage re-soldered, and I saw none inside. I shall esteem it as another favour if you send information on these points to your

Most humble servant,
V. CARDELLA, S.J.

N.B. The sooner you reply the more grateful I shall be.

This letter was, doubtless, written after Father Cardella had received Giulio's heart from Signor Santucci. The photograph mentioned in it is the one recently found in Signor Santucci's house at Mentana, by Monsignor Merry del Val, and now in his possession. It represents Giulio in full Zouave gala uniform, with a view of St. Peter's forming a background.

The breakage in the leaden tube enclosing the heart is explained in the letters that follow.

The following is Signor Pietro Santucci's reply to the above.

18th January, 1871.

Very Rev. Father,

Pardon my delay in answering your favour of the 6th inst., occasioned by my absence from home for several days, and in thanking you, together with Mr. Watts-Russell, for wishing to reward me in so courteous and generous a manner, for a work of Christian piety. I beg you to convey to him in the warmest terms, on my behalf, the deep appreciation I feel of the sentiments expressed in my regard in his most kind letter, which letter I shall ever keep by me with religious care.

I have now to tell you that the monument was damaged on the 18th of September last by a band of exiles, who, however, only broke the cross and the iron bands encircling it, leaving erect the column itself. On the 3rd of November following, the day of the famous celebration, the column was entirely overthrown, and was left lying on the ground, like all the other monuments. And it was, in truth, a most fortunate chance that it did not occur to their minds to break up the brick foundation, and that no one in the town had mentioned the fact of the precious relic lying buried under it. Uneasy and disturbed in mind at the thought of the possibility of a scandal, and a shocking profanation, I charged a workman to remove the relic to a place of safety during the night of the 3rd—4th, which was done. Not being able to do the work by himself, he secured the assistance of two others; and there was one of them who, in spite of all I could say to the contrary, allowed himself to be influenced by a disgraceful desire that, inside that tube, there might be found the whole series of Pontifical coinage, from the centesimo to the 100-franc piece; and, from a shameful persuasion of gain, he was moved to open the said leaden tube. The interior terra-cotta vessel, however, in which were enclosed the precious remains, was found sound and intact. For the rest, your Reverence was justified in thinking that the breakage could not have arisen accidentally, and that those whom you supposed to be the authors of it would not have been satisfied with so little; and indeed, I, stripped at that time of any kind of authority, could not have prevented any sacrilege attempted by them.

The bearer of this letter is one of my sons, who, through the munificence of the Holy Father, has employment in the Monte di Pietà here in Rome. To him you can hand over the photograph of the angelic Giulio, which I shall carefully keep, together with another left me by his affectionate brother, Wilfrid, when he last visited this place.

With these short, but reliable details, which you asked for, I beg you to accept a renewal of my sentiments of gratitude and esteem, and believe me,

Your Reverence's obedient servant,
PIETRO SANTUCCI.

It will be seen, in the succeeding letters, that the motive which led the workman to open the tube was kept concealed from Giulio's father and family, for fear it should cause them pain. Such secrecy is, of course, no longer necessary, and on the other hand, it is interesting to note how providentially the heart escaped the dangers of profanation that so closely menaced it.

The following letter was written by the Rev. V. Cardella, S.J., to Signor Pietro Santucci, a short time after the above had been received.

My dear Sir,

Many thanks for your most kind letter, and for the pleasure you gave me of becoming acquainted with your son.

In writing to Mr. Watts-Russell, I shall say nothing about what you have told me regarding the curiosity of the man who opened the tube. The only things I would wish to know, are (1) if inside the tube there is still a leaden box (I think it was lead); (2) if this little box was broken open to see whether there was any money inside.

Begging you to oblige me again with this information and anticipating my thanks, believe me,

Your humble servant,
V. CARDELLA, S.J.

Twenty-Seven Years Later — 1895

In reply to which Signor Pietro Santucci sent the following:—

Very Rev. Father,

In reply to your favour, there is no need for me to describe the shape of the leaden tube, since it must be sufficiently well known to you. In the interior of this leaden tube, there is another vessel of terra-cotta, the mouth of which was perfectly sealed up and tarred, and which was found, after the exhumation, sound and uninjured, not only by myself, but also by the Secretary of the Municipality, Andrew Marino, and by the doctor, Dottore Ignazio Vespignani........ The interior of the leaden tube (and all round the receptacle of terra-cotta) was filled, if I mistake not, either with bran or with sawdust. On the upper surface there was a paper (signed by someone whose name I do not remember) testifying to the heart, etc. (precordi) of Giulio being inside the terra-cotta vessel, ... and in addition, a picture of our Lady, to whose protection the precious remains were commended, with a written prayer that they might be saved from sacrilege and profanation, as in fact happened.

It is, moreover, my duty to inform you that during the night time I removed the marble column to a place of safety in my property. The monument raised to Rialan, which was in close proximity to that of Russell, is lying on the ground, but without having been damaged; and the present Municipality has, until now, given no instructions for its removal to the neighbouring church of the Pietà, as I have several times suggested. But nothing has been done, nor will anything be done, by reason of the prevailing panic.

Begging your prayers for myself and family, and with unalterable esteem,

I remain, your obedient servant,
PIETRO SANTUCCI.

The following letter was written by Signor Pietro Santucci to Father Cardella, soon after the receipt of Giulio's photograph:—

March 2nd, 1871.

Very Rev. Father,

Pardon me if I have allowed some time to go by without acknowledging having received, through my son Philip, the photograph of our most beloved Giulio Russell, together with several copies of his angelic life. I treasure both the one and the other, and will keep them most carefully. Indeed I have put the picture in a place set aside for it in our private chapel, where also reposed the body of Sta. Felicita, Martyr, which was given over to the Holy Father, as will appear from the accompanying poem, composed by the Rev. Father Angelini, S.J. I could not assign a more worthy place to the memorial of so noble and heroic a youth. And indeed, who knows but that our Lord may some day permit him also to be venerated on the altar? And I hope, moreover, that through his intercession my family may one day be in some way compensated for the plunder, pillage, and other immense losses we have suffered in these sad times.

I renew sentiments of the deepest respect and gratitude, and believe me,

Your most obedient servant,
PIETRO SANTUCCI.

A week after the above was written, Father Cardella wrote the following letter to Signor Pietro Santucci:—

March 11th.

Dear Sir,

Yesterday, at last, I sent the tube to Mr. Watts-Russell, in England. In writing to him I said that the two men who assisted the person employed by Signor Santucci, very much to his displeasure, opened the tube out of curiosity, but I did not mention that this curiosity was in order to see if there was any money inside. Such a piece of news would have caused him pain and annoyance. I beg Signor Pietro Santucci, if, in the future, any opportunity occurs to him of speaking either with Giulio's father or brother, not to enter into any further detail regarding the curiosity of the two who opened the tube. I have also said in my letter that Signor Pietro has had the goodness to place the little column in a place of safety. I suppose the cross has been broken to pieces, and that those pieces will never be found.

Renewing my thanks, I sign myself,

>Your most humble and devoted servant,
>   V. CARDELLA, S.J.

It is rather to be regretted, for the sake of this Memoir, that Father Cardella did not mention by whom he sent the tube, containing Giulio's heart, to England. However, it is satisfactory to know that it reached the Rev. M. Watts-Russell's hands safely after all the dangers it had passed through. As we have already seen, it was ultimately forwarded to the Carmelite Convent at Darlington; and I am certain that my readers will agree that no more fitting resting place could be allotted to the heart of the young hero than that it now occupies, in the choir, under the statue of Our Lady, to whom he showed such love and devotion while in life, and whose protection saved it from the profanation it might easily have suffered at Mentana.

These are all the letters found at Mentana in Signor Filippo Santucci's possession, and, as I said before, it is from them I have derived much of the knowledge I now possess regarding the circumstances attending the saving of Giulio's heart. The story of its actual rescue, as told in Chapter I., I learned from a letter written to me by Signor Santucci, dictated by Dottore Vespignani, of Mentana, who was, probably, the only man alive able to give an accurate account of that romantic episode. Other details, which he omitted, were supplied me by Miss Watts-Russell. There is no need to publish these letters here, since the story, as told in Chapter I., is practically a copy of them.

But I wish to include in this Chapter two interesting letters, and an extract from a third, written soon after Giulio's death—letters quite recently found among papers kept by the Reverend Mother of Carmel House, Darlington. Copies of them were kindly sent me by Miss Watts-Russell, with permission to use them as I pleased. Their existence had been quite unknown to her prior to their accidental discovery.

The first is a letter from Giulio's father written from Lourdes to one of the nuns of Darlington very soon after his noble son's death. It runs as follows:—

Lourdes, Dec. 1st, 1867.

Dear Sister N.,

I must myself thank you for your more than kind letter of sympathy, but, indeed, I have no need to be consoled. I confess that my feelings are all happiness and exultation, whenever I think of the signal grace which God has bestowed on my noble boy. I do not think I can answer your kindness in a manner more acceptable, than by relating to you one or two things, which will show you that Giulio's heroic death has a very particular relation to your holy community at Darlington. You may remember how you were good enough to lend me the MSS. of Mother Margaret Mostyn, from which I made copious extracts; and Giulio copied into his book some of these prayers—the prayer to the Guardian Angel, the prayer to Our Lady for the conversion of England, ending with the words, "England, thy dowry that was lost is brought back to thee again;" these he used daily, also the long "protestation of homage to the Blessed Virgin Mary," which contains particular petitions to be delivered from temptations at the hour of death, a promise of sundry acts of devotion to Our Blessed Lady—especially that he would say this prayer every Saturday on his knees,—a resolution to carry this protestation about his person both living and dying, and a request that it might be buried with him, as a testimony of defiance against the devil, etc. On looking over his prayer-book last summer, and asking him about this prayer, which is *very long*, I was astonished to hear that he said it *every day*, and the way in which the pages are soiled testifies to the truth of it. See how literally all his petitions have been answered! His death must have been instantaneous, for he was shot through the brain, so that temptations had no opportunity of disturbing his soul; the book was found on the field where it had dropped from him, or been cast aside by the wretched people, who stole from his person all that they thought worth taking. When I came to Rome, the book was put into my hands; he had already been buried many days, but Our Lady so arranged that by an extraordinary permission of the Cardinal Vicar, the coffin was again opened, and I had an opportunity of placing a copy of this prayer upon his breast. Thus, you see, you may almost claim Giulio as a brother, for his soul was nurtured upon the same sweet devotions as yours and your sisters in religion. Ellen will write you other details.

Say everything most kind for me to the Rev. Mother, and believe me,

Yours most faithfully in Jesus and Mary,

M. WATTS-RUSSELL.

P.S.—We were charmed with the long extract you gave Ellen from Mr. Burke's letter. There is one from his old tutor, Arthur Marshall, the author of a book, which is just now making such a sensation, *The Comedy of Convocation*: "My sorrow is almost as great as your own, for if I had lost my own son, I could hardly have felt it more. When I first read of it in the newspaper, it seemed to me impossible. Let me grieve with you. I do not feel the joy I ought to feel at another martyr being added to the roll of saints, for I am much too human to be comforted by great thoughts. What I do feel is, that the best boy that ever lived, and one whom I loved with as much affection as I ever felt for any human being, is gone from you and me. I knew him almost as well as you did, and I look upon his death as the sacrifice of a choice victim required by God, for some purpose of mercy to those who survive."

The prayer of protestation of homage to Our Lady, mentioned in this letter, is the one already spoken of (page 49), and replaced in Giulio's grave by me on May 26th of this year. Mr. Watts-Russell is justified in calling it *very long*. The extract given in the biography (page 88) is not half of it. Before placing it in the grave, I took a copy of it, and it filled five pages of ordinary note paper, pretty closely written. In the part omitted in the biography, some of the sentiments are wonderfully fine. Especially noteworthy is clear reference in it to the Immaculate Conception, which is mentioned in express terms. If the prayer was composed, as stated, by Mother Margaret Mostyn (who died about the time of Cromwell), it affords splendid testimony of the belief in the Immaculate Conception held some 200 years ago. The manuscript prayerbook, in which Giulio copied it together with other prayers, was picked up off the battlefield, I believe, by one of the Pontifical soldiers, who handed it to Captain Shee. It passed from his hands to the possession of Mrs. Stone, from whom Mr. Watts-Russell received it on his arrival in Rome shortly after Giulio's death. It is now in the possession of the Rev. M. Watts-Russell, Giulio's surviving brother.[14]

I now pass on to a letter written, at the same time as the above, by Giulio's sister to the same Religious of Darlington. It is interesting, as it describes with a certain amount of detail the ceremony held in the Campo Verano in Rome, when Giulio's body was exhumed and exposed to view for the consolation of his father, sister, and brother, November 23rd, 1867:—

Lourdes, 1st December, 1867.

My dearest Sister N.,

I do not know how to thank you for your most dear letter, it gave me such pleasure. We have felt more joy than sorrow in dear Giulio's death; we cannot mourn, death has been a triumph. The first notice we saw of it was in a French news-

---

14 At the moment I am writing this, Giulio's MS. prayerbook is, temporarily, in my possession, having been lent me by Father Watts-Russell. Some of the prayers in it are, I am told, composed by his father.

paper. We almost expected *one* to be taken—I do not know why, and we anxiously examined every paper, to find a list of the dead; but they would not publish the list. We found, however, his death spoken of before the list appeared. That was on the 13th, at Marseilles. We had taken our places on board the express steamer, which was leaving for Cività Vecchia, as we found it impossible to get a comfortable apartment in Spain, and the prices were extravagant. We were anxious to see the brothers, after all they had gone through. I was rejoicing at the pleasure of giving them a surprise, as we had not written to tell them of our arrival, when dear Giulio's death changed, for a while, our joy into grief. I felt his death just at first; but even then it was mingled with joy. But my joy has been wonderfully increased at seeing, once more, the sacred body in Rome, twenty days after his glorious death. The Cardinal Vicar gave permission; this was Father Cardella's doing; Papa would not have asked such a favour. Giulio's body was disinterred and brought to the church, where Mass was said. We all went to Holy Communion. After Mass, the "Libera" was said. The body was then taken back to be buried, Papa, Wilfrid, and two nuns carrying torches. The Jesuit Father began the "Te Deum." He said the "Gloria Patri," instead of the "Requiem," and the "Laudate;" it was a glorious funeral. What was most consoling was to see the state of the body. I could not have believed the suppleness of all his limbs, had I not seen it; you could not realize that he was dead. His hands, every joint of his fingers, bent like those of a person in life; his head moved about with the slightest touch. Many were present, among others five nuns. They all said, on seeing the Jesuit Father take up his head, "Let us kiss it;" but he said "No;" so that, though I wished to kiss his hand, I did not do so, as the Jesuit Father had said "No" to the nuns. I touched my rosary on his face. His face was a little discoloured, and his eye, which was open, was rather sunk; but there was beauty and innocence in that face. We all felt so happy. In Rome he is regarded as a saint. Numbers ask for a souvenir of him—the Cardinal Vicar, the General of the Passionists, numbers of Jesuits, and monks and nuns of other Orders. The Cardinal Vicar requested Monsignor Geneste to draw up a statement of the many little facts, which he would give to the Holy Father to read, and which might serve, possibly, for the process of his canonization at some future time.

When the body was disinterred from the common grave at Monte Rotondo, to be transported to Rome, several of his comrades were standing by. One said, "Voilà l'innocence même;" another, "Nous n'avons jamais entendu de sa bouche une parole legère;" a third, "Nobody is in heaven, if he is not there." A French Priest followed the body on foot, out of devotion, from Monte Rotondo to Rome, 15 miles; he also *wished* to pay the expenses of embalming the body. The heart and brains were without any taint of corruption on the fourteenth day after his death. It seems to me a pity that they should then have been put into spirits. I send you a piece of linen stained with his blood.

Your affectionate child,
ELLEN WATTS-RUSSELL.

The Cardinal Vicar, who gave leave for the exhumation of Giulio's body, was Cardinal Patrizi. I have been told that his having requested Monsignor Geneste to draw up a statement on Giulio's character, with a view to his possible canonization, is the strongest argument in favour of his sanctity; his Eminence being of a most unenthusiastic temperament, and requiring clear evidence of facts before accepting them.

The third letter, of which the following is an extract, was written by the Countess of Montgelas to Giulio's father, shortly after Christmas, 1867. I give it, as showing what a powerful influence Giulio had upon people, and especially upon those of the poorer classes. I believe his love of the poor was quite extraordinary.

"I did not tell you of the solemn Requiem Mass Max (*i.e.*, her husband) had said for Giulio; it was far grander than the one I had said for him, all the church being decorated with flowers and draperies. The people came from all the neighbourhood. The Curé preached upon Giulio. What strikes me very much, is the way this Christmas has been kept. The Curé is quite astonished at it; it had never been so before, and he has been Parish Priest 36 years. Nearly the whole flock approached the Sacraments. The poor old Curé was quite exhausted, having sat immovable in the confessional from five o'clock in the morning until seven in the evening for several days, only taking time to say his Mass and get some dinner; and he was half frozen, too, for the cold is dreadful, and he is 72 and feeble. He does not know what to attribute this change to, and had he known he would have sent for help. But I know the reason:—*Julian passed there.*"

The letter from which this extract is taken was written from Egglkofen in Bavaria, where the Count and Countess de Montgelas had a country place. It appears that Wilfrid and Giulio spent a short time there, not long before they entered the ranks of the Zouaves. During their visit they were constantly associated with the peasantry, among whom, it would seem, they carried on a little apostolate. At any rate, they completely won their hearts.

I have now to place before my readers a letter written to myself in French, by no less a person than the Chevalier Geneste, of whom mention is made in the pages of this biography. He was a great friend of the Watts-Russell family, and for some time, I believe, acted as tutor to Wilfrid and Giulio in Rome. It will be better, however, as I have a few words to say about this gentleman, to devote a separate chapter to him and his letter.

CHAPTER V.

Monsieur le Chevalier de Geneste—Relics of Giulio found in his possession—Giulio's blood-stained jacket, and Wilfrid's diary of the year 1868—Monsieur de Geneste's letter to myself, June 1894.

IT was quite by chance, so to speak, that I found out that Monsieur de Geneste was still living. I had been working on Giulio's account some four months, before receiving information that he was not only alive, but residing in Rome, in the Via S. Martino ai Monti. Two days after hearing this I paid him a visit, hoping to obtain of him important details regarding our hero. Nor was I disappointed. Such interesting information did he give me, that I requested him to commit all his experiences regarding Giulio to writing. This he did in the form of a letter addressed to myself, which I am now about to submit to my readers.

But before doing so, I must make mention of two most interesting and important discoveries I made in his house. The first was Giulio's blood-stained Zouave jacket, *i.e.*, the one he wore at Mentana. I felt the greatest possible satisfaction at finding this relic, especially because in a letter, written to me some months previous by the Rev. M. Watts-Russell, he told me that the jacket had been lost, and that, so far as he or his sister were concerned, there was no trace of it. I found the jacket rather moth-eaten, but otherwise intact. The blood stains were well marked, especially on the sleeve and round the neck, but, of course, they had considerably faded. The other discovery was involved in that of the jacket, for while I was inspecting the garment, Monsieur de Geneste's daughter came forward with a little book, which she placed in my hands, saying it had been found in the pocket of the jacket. On opening it I found it to be a diary written in pencil, and my first impression was that I had lighted upon another most interesting relic of Giulio. A diary kept by himself, as a Zouave, could not fail to be a most valuable object. On closer inspection, however, I found in it references to himself which excluded the possibility of his being the author of it; and soon it became evident that it was a diary kept by Wilfrid in 1868, the year following that of Giulio's death. Wilfrid's opinion of his younger brother's sanctity may be judged from the following entries:—"*November 3rd*, Anniversary of Holy Giulio's death at Mentana, Gloria in excelsis Deo, et in terra nobis pax." "*November 23rd.* Anniversary of Holy Giulio's 3rd burial, when Papa and Ellen and I saw him in his coffin. Holy Giulio, pray for us." Several times throughout the diary, Giulio is invoked in this way, and his name hardly ever appears without the prefix "Holy."

Some interesting information also may be derived from the book. For instance, towards the end, there is a list of events of 1867, from which we learn that the two brothers entered the Zouaves on June 5th of that year; so that Giulio's term of service was only five months. A few pages further still, I found a little pencil drawing executed by Giulio. It had been cut out from some other book, and pasted in. It represented an abbey ruin—evidently an English scene, possibly in the neighbourhood of Ushaw College, where he spent two years. The author's name was written in full in the corner of the picture, the execution of which showed considerable talent. There were other specimens of his drawings in the book, consisting of the heads of Mr. John Bright, Mr. Disraeli, Mr. Gladstone, Earl Derby, and Lord Russell, all very well done.

Monsieur de Geneste allowing me to retain this diary, I placed it in the hands of Father Watts-Russell soon after my arrival in England from Rome. It would have given me much pleasure to have been able to hand the jacket over to him as well; but Monsieur de Geneste would not allow it out of his sight, and I had no courage to ask him to let me take it with me to England. However, I trust the relic may some day find its way to Giulio's surviving relatives, who, beyond doubt, have prior right to its possession.

According to Monsieur de Geneste's own testimony, the jacket has never been out of his keeping since Giulio's death. He says he took it off the body himself, when he brought it to Rome from Monte Rotondo, since which he has never parted with it. This statement ill accords with the assertions of some of the nuns of Carmel House, Darlington, namely, that the jacket was brought to the convent by Giulio's father, and allowed to remain there for a day and night; nor is it easily reconcilable with Father Watts-Russell's testimony that his brother Wilfrid had it in his possession during his lifetime. These conflicting accounts would lead me to doubt that the garment now possessed by Monsieur de Geneste was, in reality, Giulio's jacket, were it not for Wilfrid's diary having been found in the pocket. Under the circumstances, the only conclusion to be arrived at regarding the matter is that Monsieur de Geneste's memory has failed him in this particular. Nevertheless, it should be remembered that there were two jackets to be disposed of as relics a blood-stained one and the gala one, which was on the body when lying for three days in Monsieur de Geneste's house. What became of the latter jacket is not known, but it is possible that Wilfrid took possession of it, and that by some confusion it was thought he had the other. This explanation, however, has no reference to the statement made by the nuns of Darlington; those who saw the jacket, brought for their inspection, have a distinct recollection of the bloodstains on it, and other details.

I now come to Monsieur de Geneste's letter, which is so interesting that it ought not to be omitted. Much of what he relates has already been told in the biography, but not always very accurately, so that I have no hesitation in introducing the repetition. The letter was written in French, but I give it in English for the sake of greater convenience.

Twenty-Seven Years Later — 1895

Reverend Father,

Now that his Eminence the Cardinal Vicar, and Monsignore the Secretary of the Vicariate have strongly advised us to collect all possible evidence regarding our young friend, Julian Watts-Russell, ex-Pontifical Zouave, I no longer hesitate to put you in possession of all I can testify regarding him.

As I have already told you personally, I knew him as a child, and I can affirm, with all truth, that I never came across any child who united in his person so many qualities as were to be observed in him. To say nothing of his physique, which was most attractive, everything about him had a drawing influence upon people. It was enough to approach him for a moment to love him. He was noted for a sweetness that was quite angelic, and for a disposition that was always even. Never was there to be seen in him any motion of anger or impatience. If he happened occasionally to have some dispute with his brother Wilfrid (whose character was quite opposed to Julian's), he invited him immediately to kneel down and join him in an act of contrition, after which they would rise, shake hands, and embrace each other.

When he came with his brother to enlist in the Pontifical Zouaves, he was influenced by a settled resolution—I will say more—by an ardent desire to give his life in defence of the Pope and the Holy See. It is this which explains his constant perseverance in the religious exercises he imposed on himself in his civil life.

His worthy and noble father, Mr. Michael Watts-Russell, when about to leave his dear children, to return to England, did me the honour of confiding them to my care. I promised him I would treat them as my own children; and, in fact, from that moment I looked upon them as part of my family, and God, the searcher of hearts, knows well what I would have done for their good, as He knows what was the depth of my grief at the news of the death of young Julian.

At the time when Wilfrid and Julian joined the Pontifical army, I lived in the Via Quattro Fontane, my house being surrounded by a garden. Our young volunteers were fond of coming there whenever they were at liberty. It was a real pleasure to see them amusing themselves there; Julian, especially, was quite remarkable for his child-like gaiety. I cannot remember to have ever seen him depressed or uneasy; and indeed, the beautiful motto he had adopted clearly proves that he had only one thing at heart, namely, to love God. "Anima mia, anima mia, ama Dio e tira via!"—"My soul, my soul, love God and go thy way!" I remember also having heard him, several times, express himself thus: "I cannot understand what pleasure men can find in offending God."

The eve of the battle of Mentana, in 1867, young Julian came to me in the morning. Saluting me, he said, "Good day, Monsieur de Geneste, I have come to take dinner with you for the last time." "How is that?" I asked. "Do my dinners no longer please you?" "Oh no!" he said, "it is not that, I mean to say that, to-morrow, I shall be one of the first killed, and shall go to Heaven." He then commissioned me to tell the news to his father. On my saying, in reply to this, "The Lord save me from having to deliver such news to him," he replied, "What!

do you think Papa will grieve so much? On the contrary, he will thank God. Ellen (his sister) will cry a little; but our Lord will comfort her." And, in very truth, the tears shed for Julian were rather tears of consolation than of sorrow.

The dinner hour having come, he insisted on seating himself at the table between my little son, aged four years, and daughter, two-and-a-half years old. He kissed them on the forehead several times, saying to them in Italian, "Keep yourself always pure and innocent, my little friends, and we shall meet in heaven; for I am going there to-morrow."

After dinner he took leave of us, saying he would meet us again in heaven; Madame de Geneste and children, in order to see him longer, climbed up to the top of a wall which faced the Via Quattro Fontane. They threw him two oranges, plucked from an orange tree close by. Julian stooped to pick them up, and on raising himself, shouted to them, "In heaven we shall eat much better ones than these." He then gave them another salute with his hand, and pointing to heaven a last time, disappeared.

The morning after the battle, a Monsignore, whose name I do not now remember,[15] came to tell me of the heroic death of my young friend Julian, and invited me to accompany him to Monte Rotondo, in order to get possession of the body and bring it to Rome. We started at once. On reaching Monte Rotondo, we went to the cemetery, where young Julian had already been buried. We disinterred the body as soon as possible, and made all arrangements for conveying

---

15   Monsignor de Geneste thinks it was Monsignor Talbot.

it to Rome, and to my house. It was in my house that it was embalmed, and not at Monte Rotondo, as has been erroneously stated.

I had the heart and lungs removed, and I enclosed them myself in a crystal phial . . . . . containing . . . . . spirits of wine. I wished to be able to hand over the relic to Mr. Watts-Russell in a good state of preservation.

The process of embalming being finished, I hastened to gather up the blood which was flowing from the wound in his right eye. I soaked it up with wadding, which I now keep as a precious relic. I cut off some of his hair, and carefully washed his precious body.

After that I re-clothed it in his gala Zouave dress, and laid it out on an ornamental couch, which I had taken care to prepare in a large parlour on the ground floor. I placed a crown of white roses round his brow, and round his neck I put the scapular of our Blessed Lady, also a crucifix and a palm in his hands. It remained exposed like this for three days. People came from all parts of the city to see this "Angeletto," as they called him. They kissed his hands and his feet, and they touched him with objects of devotion, such as medals, rosaries, pictures, etc.

One could scarcely help being moved to tears at the sight of this young soldier of seventeen years, who had generously given his life for the defence of the Church and the Vicar of Jesus Christ. He seemed to be in a sweet sleep. The smile on his lips imparted a supernatural expression to his countenance. The wound in the right eye, and the bruises on the forehead, served to bring out in greater prominence the beauty of his face.

I keep as a precious relic his blood-stained jacket, *i.e.*, the one he wore on the battlefield when he was killed. What numbers of people have venerated it!

What was quite marvellous was that, when on the third day we proceeded to place the body of our young friend in the zinc coffin, we found it as flexible as on the first day; a circumstance which made us hope it would remain always sound. Alas! our hopes in this matter have not been realized, on account of a small opening having formed in the zinc coffin, which gave entrance to the water, resulting in the total decomposition of the body. This is all the more to be deplored, inasmuch as there are a thousand probabilities to one that we shall some day see him venerated on the altar.

On the Friday evening, the body was conveyed on a funeral car to the English College, and was there solemnly received at the door by the students in procession and, at their head, the new Rector, the Rev. Father O'Callaghan, of the Oblates of St. Charles in London; and on the Saturday morning the Office and Mass were sung, at which many persons of rank, ecclesiastic and lay, assisted, as well as several fellow soldiers of the deceased. In the evening, it was solemnly carried to the cemetery of San Lorenzo, and was buried in a place of distinction. His brother Wilfrid laid on the grave two wreaths, made of flowers picked in the Pope's garden, praying, at the same time, for the repose of the soul of his beloved Julian, who, let us hope, now possesses, in Heaven, the crown of the just, and the martyr's palm.

The following inscription was placed on his tombstone:—

HEIC AD MARTYRUM CRYPTAS
DORMIT IN PACE
JULIANUS WATTS-RUSSELL, MICHAELIS F.,
ANGLUS CLARO GENERE.
PRO PETRI SEDE STRENUE DIMICANS
IN ACIE AD NOMENTUM OCCUBUIT
III. NON. NOVEMB. ANNO MDCCCLXVII.
AN. N. XVII., MENSS X.
ADOLESCENS CHRISTI MILES,
VIVE IN DEO.

Young Julian Watts-Russell, instead of being 21 years of age, as stated in Father Cardella's little biography, was only 17; a circumstance which attaches more merit, in the eyes of God and the world, to his sacrifice. Many of his companions, whom I knew, expressed their deep regret at not having shared his lot, attributing it to their own unworthiness. They frankly confessed that their young fellow-soldier, Julian, had in his countenance and bearing something not easily described, which commanded respect and love. Every time I myself was in his company, I experienced the same feeling. My affection for him equalled the respect he had inspired in me from the first moment of my acquaintance with him.

"Happy father," I often exclaimed, "to have such a son!" Everything about him breathed forth truth, innocence and holiness. All during the time it was permitted to me to be in his company, I cannot recollect to have heard, in any of his sayings, any word which was either light or out of place. He always weighed what he said, in order to commit no fault against charity or propriety. These reflections, or rather convictions, of mine were those also of my wife and children, the latter of whom, in spite of their tender years, could already appreciate his even temperament and angelic sweetness. It was quite a festivity for them when he came to our house.

I hope, Reverend Father, that the particulars I have thought it my duty to give you concerning our young hero may be of use for the new biography you propose to publish. You may rely on me for a French and Italian translation. Such a publication ought to be spread abroad as much as possible, in order that the deeper acquaintance with this angelic youth therefrom arising may induce young men of his age to imitate him faithfully, and become saints like him.

With deepest respect, believe me, dear Rev. Father,

>	Yours very sincerely in Jesus, Mary and Joseph,
>		J. EDOUARD GENESTE,
>	Chevalier of S. Gregory the Great.

Rome, June 24, 1894.

P.S.—I forgot to mention two things concerning our young hero, which appear to me to be very important. No sooner had the news of his beloved son's death reached the ears of Mr. Michael Watts-Russell, who was then in Spain, than he started at once for Rome, with his daughter Ellen. They arrived there early in November, and the Reverend Father Cardella, who well knew what pleasure it would have given them to see again the dear angel, whose body had preserved all its flexibility, obtained leave from the Vicariate to exhume it. This was on November 23rd—just twenty days after his death. What must not have been the consolation of the father, sister, brother, and certain friends of the deceased to see the body again, and accompany it to the cemetery church, where was celebrated the Holy Sacrifice of the Mass, at which all received Holy Communion. At the end, the dear remains were conveyed back to the grave, and Mr. Watts-Russell and his daughter left next morning, their hearts consoled and their souls delighted at having found the body of dear Julian as flexible as if he was still living.

A few days after their departure, I obtained a private audience of the Holy Father, Pius IX. of holy memory. His Holiness, in that audience, made me give him a full account of all I knew concerning the young volunteer Julian, his brother Wilfrid, and that noble English family. No sooner had the Holy Father heard the events concerning Julian, and, in particular, his last visit to me in the Via Quattro Fontane, and all the incidents preceding and accompanying his heroic death, than he exclaimed with much emotion: "He will be the Guerin of England." The Holy Father said that, because he knew that it was I that caused Guerin to leave Ancona in 1860, and that I had been as well acquainted with him as with Julian. I looked upon these words of the Holy Father as prophetic, and, from that moment, I never had any doubt but that we should some day see this dear angel venerated on the Altar. May this come about. Amen.

I have a few remarks and comments to make on the information furnished by this letter. In the first place, the allusion to the Cardinal Vicar and the Secretary of the Vicariate, with which the letter opens, has reference to a visit Monsieur de Geneste and I paid them together in June last, with a view to informing them of the work recently done on Giulio's account, and placing before them some of the testimony that had come to hand about him. Both his Eminence and the Secretary were much interested, and urged us to continue collecting information.

The next item in the letter, about which I have a remark to make, is the description of Giulio's last visit to Monsieur de Geneste's house. In speaking with me on this last scene, Monsieur de Geneste added to what he has committed to writing, another little circumstance worth mentioning, namely, that Giulio on this occasion was in the highest possible spirits at the prospect of falling in battle the following day. He was always in a happy mood; but on this day he was unusually hilarious, even apparently to being boisterous. The whole story affords fairly convincing evidence, not only of the spirit with which Giulio was animated in offering himself as a Pontifical soldier, but also that he had a clear presentiment of his death. In his mind, there was no doubt as to what would happen to him next day; it was not mere probability, it was certainty. His conduct can only be satisfactorily explained on this supposition. To my mind, his high sanctity makes it quite reasonable to believe that he had a supernatural foreknowledge of his death; for we know that God Almighty is very near to them that are generous in His service, and reveals things to children and the pure of heart that He hides from all others. And what generosity to God can exceed the desire of shedding one's blood in defence of His Church.

Monsieur de Geneste testifies to Giulio's body being embalmed in his house in the Via Quattro Fontane, and corrects a statement that the embalming took place in the cemetery of Monte Rotondo. That statement was made by Captain Shee, who assisted in the exhumation of the body when Monsieur de Geneste arrived at Monte Rotondo to claim it. He remembers that the body, before being taken away, was laid in the mortuary chapel and there subjected to some operation, performed by a doctor, whom Monsieur de Geneste had brought with him. This operation, which he himself witnessed, consisted in cutting open the body, and after certain organs had been removed, stuffing it with tow and arsenic; and he mistook it for a rough process of embalming, whereas it was merely a measure taken to check immediate decomposition, until the real embalming could be performed.

I have something to add to Monsieur de Geneste's testimony regarding the numbers that came to see Giulio's body, when it was laid out in his house. Among the visitors was an English doctor—a Protestant. He came the first day out of curiosity. But the aspect of the body so attracted and moved him, that he frequently returned to see it during those three days, and finally could scarcely tear himself away from it. Not long afterwards he became a Catholic! This I have on the authority of Monsieur de Geneste, who, unfortunately, fails to remember the doctor's name, although he bears in mind that he resided a very short distance from his own house. This is by no means the only grace obtained through Giulio's intercession since his glorious death. I have in my possession written evidence of other remarkable graces, almost amounting to miracles, obtained by having recourse to his intercession; the written testimony being supplied by the persons who have been so favoured. I have no hesitation in affirming that there is ground for attributing miraculous properties to his blood, since pieces of linen stained with it have been, apparently, applied to sick persons with astonishing effect.[16]

This letter, and my comments on it, bring my task to a conclusion for the present. The labour and time spent in compiling the matter herein published will by no means have been spent in vain, if this memoir of Giulio's becomes, in consequence, more widely spread. As I said before, my principal object in committing to writing the events of this year in connection with Giulio, is to procure that the fame of his sanctity may be spread far and wide, not only for the sake of the benefit of his example, but also that wholesome conclusions may be arrived at in regard to the question of the temporal sovereignty of the Vicar of Christ from the evident workings of God's grace in this favoured soul.

---

16   I have evidence of this in one case.

The late Bishop Chadwick, in one of his pastorals, made reference in the warmest terms to the Zouaves who had fallen in defence of the Holy See. He did not hesitate to call them martyrs, nor to style their intercession as powerful. I feel justified here in appropriating the words he used about them in general to Giulio in particular: "Let us cherish his memory, and if there be any among you who had the happiness of having been intimate with that glorious martyr, bless God for having vouchsafed to you so great a grace, and fear not to invoke his powerful intercession."

FINIS.

Twenty-Seven Years Later — 1895

Grave of Julian Watts-Russell, taken in 1894.

LIST OF SUBSCRIBERS

TO THE FUND FOR THE RESTORATION OF GIULIO'S GRAVE AND MONUMENT.

The Hon. and Most Rev. Monsignor Stonor.
The Hon. and Rt. Rev. Monsignor Stanley.
The Rt. Rev. Monsignor Giles.
The Rt. Rev. Monsignor de Stacpoole.
The Very Rev. Monsignor Merry del Val.
The Very Rev. Monsignor O'Bryen.
The Very Rev. Monsignor Dunn.
The Very Rev. J. Bannin, P.S.M.
The Very Rev. Thomas Belton, C.R.L.
The Very Rev. M. Watts-Russell, X.I.P.
The Rev. J. Prior, D.D.
The Rev. G. Phillips and a Friend.
The Rev. A. Hinsley, D.D.
The Rev. G. Tatum, M.A.
The Rev. Kenelm Vaughan.
The Rev. Claud Lindsay.
The Rev. Students of the English College.

Alderman Sir Stuart Knill, Bart.
Lady Herbert of Lea.
The Lady Ellenborough.
The Lady Frances Lindsay.
Mr. and Mrs. P. Watts-Russell.
Miss E. Watts-Russell.
Mrs. Meynell.
Mrs. George Vaughan.
E. Granville Ward, Esq.
C. W. Worlledge, Esq.
William Cagger, Esq.
Carlyle Spedding, Esq.
Charles Astor Bristed, Esq.
W. Osborne Christmas, Esq.
James Coventry, Esq.
Captain Shee.
Dr. Eyre.

APPENDIX.

THE following Appendix is original to this republished addition. It contains additional relevant material to Julian Watts-Russell that the reader will find beneficial for learning more and appreciating the heroic sacrice and characther of Julian.

INTERVIEW WITH JULIAN'S CONFESSOR FATHER ARMELLINI, S.J.

March 17, 1894.

NO sort of difficulty attaches to a visit to Father Armellini, S.J.[17] He lives in the Via del Seminario at the Palazzo Borromeo, become, after many phases of transformation, the Gregorian University, and known, by antonomasy, as the Roman College. It is only a question of finding the room he occupies, either east or west among the many who live there, and of making the porter sure of your integrity. Thus the supernumerary porters are dispensed from running on multitudinous errands. The house is the residence of the Roman Provincial, the teaching fathers forming only a nucleus of the community.

Father Armellini was at home, and at once most graciously acceded to my request for an interview, and spontaneously gave me a most interesting account of all that he remembered about Julian Watts-Russell.

"You had more to do with Julian Watts-Russell during

---

17   The postulator of the cause of the English Martyrs.

his stay in Italy, than any other priest, not excepting even Father Cardella, who, for the rest, may be considered more in the light of a friend than as his spiritual father?"

"Yes," he said, "I had to do with Julian and his brothers from the beginning. They were three and they came to live in the College of Nobles,[18] in this very house, where they stayed something more than a year. I was their confessor then and afterwards; and I retain the most gratifying remembrances of our relations.

"One day I was informed that two of the pious youths had determined to become Zouaves in the Papal army. The third, as you all know, became a Passionist father."

"But your connection with them did not end here?"

"No, I continued to see both the young soldiers frequently afterwards. When the time of war came, they were then stationed in the barracks, which were then, as now, in the Castle of St. Angelo. Providing against a possible revolt, which might have been feared from the Garibaldian emissaries, but which did not actually take place, General Kanzler had divided the city into five quarters, and forbidden all intercommunication effectually securing his regulation by placing troops on the bridges and other points of vantage.

This regulation prevented Julian from coming to make his last confession to me, as he had intended to do. He told his brother that he went instead to the neighbouring Carmelite

---

18   Many English youths of the best families have belonged to this College, and in particular, the memory of the late Bishop Clifton is still fresh. The Church where they performed their spiritual exercises adjoins the College, and it is dedicated to St. Malo the Breton, and is recorded from the days of Cæcus Camerarius (A.D. 1192).

Church of Santa Maria in Traspontina. I may add that his brother, being then unwell, was not called into active service for the battle of Mentana. It is, therefore, regrettable, from my point of view, that I had not an opportunity of blessing a solemn farewell. My personal recollections after are less directly concerned with Julian. But I may tell you that it was noticed at the time that his death was caused by a shot in the eye, and it was also remembered that an English member of the Garibaldian army—a newspaper correspondent, I believe—was a crack shot who delighted in shooting his victims in the eye. He shot from the window of a house in Mentana, and thus had the advantage of resting his gun upon the window-sill, in any case Julian's suffering must have been of short duration, as he died at the end of the battle and in close proximity to the village.

"When the news of the victory was brought me, I received a visit from a pious French gentleman, whose name I do not well remember at this moment, who wished me to break the news of Julian's death to his brother. I was naturally reluctant, but finally ceded to his wish. We went together to the Castle of St. Angelo. When I broke the sad news, the youth burst into tears. I tried to comfort him, saying: 'Do not weep, your brother is most certainly a martyr.' This he at once recognized and then smiled, and quickly added: 'Still, let us pray for his dear soul.' We all knelt and said the *De Profundis* for the repose of the youthful martyr."

"This was the most optimistic and yet the truest view of the case."

"Yes, and it was the view taken by Julian's most exemplary Christian father. He was at Marseilles when the news came, and he said, with the spirit of true Christian paternity, that he had ten children, he would be willing that they should all be thus gloriously sacrificed in so holy a cause."

"And your general recollection of Julian?"

"My general recollection is of a truly candid youth, marvellously energetic for the cause of God and the spiritual life, a mere youth, it is true, but endowed with a certain earnestness, which had for its object his own spiritual advancement, and which seemed to foretoken the great glory of his end. In this way he seemed old beyond his years, and his life seemed to be conformed to the manner of his death."

THE LOCATION OF JULIAN'S GRAVE

Before republishing this book, it was the desire of the editor to document the current state of Julian's grave at Campo Verano and to provide its precise location so that the faithful on pilgrimage to Rome might pay homage to Julian and visit some of the other graves of the Papal Zouaves.

Unfortunately, after consulting the cemetery office, the staff were unable to locate the specific position of the grave, claiming that no record of it existed. This may be the result of Allied bombing that damaged the cemetery and destroyed the management office during the Second World War, or perhaps it was simply due to mismanagement over the course of one hundred and fifty years. Whatever the reason, this greatly hindered efforts to locate the grave prior to the republishing of this edition.

However, the location of the grave can reasonably be estimated as being in the vicinity of a monument constructed in 1868 dedicated to the Papal soldiers who fell in battle defending the Papal States during the Campaign of 1867 against Garibaldi and his Red Shirts. This can be deduced for several reasons. Blessed Pius IX visited the monument in 1869, along with several tombs of the Papal Zouaves, including that of Julian Watts-Russell.[19] It stands to reason that if the Holy Father visited both the monument and the graves of numerous fallen Papal Zouaves, these would have been situated within the same area.

Furthermore, the photograph we possess of the grave from 1895 shows a staggered wall behind it. That same material and design match the wall surrounding the cemetery near the street just behind the monument. An aerial view from Google Maps of the graves in that area reveals numerous markers of the same rectangular shape and construction as Julian's.

While it is disappointing that the exact site of the grave could not be rediscovered before the first edition of *England's Last Crusader*, the editor is confident that one should be able to find it with relative ease by examining the markers behind the 1867 Campaign monument near the wall by the street. Upon the discovery of the grave, a new edition of *England's Last Crusader* will be published featuring an image of its current state and precise location. To stay informed regarding the location of the grave, please visit PapalZouave.com or email papalzouavehistory@gmail.com.

---

19   *Dundalk Democrat*. February 20, 1869.

The 1867 Campaign Monument at Campo Verano Cemetary.

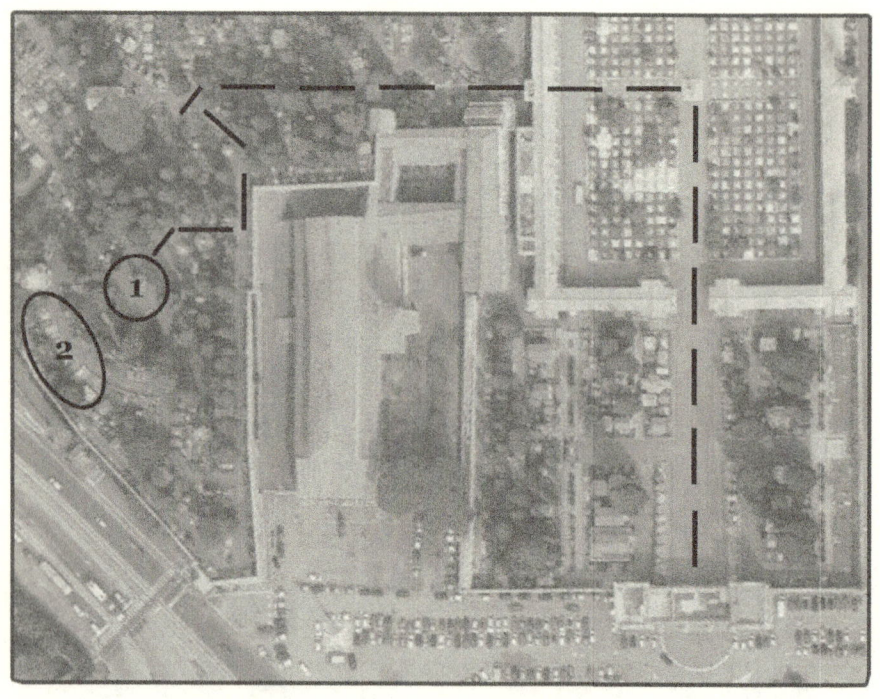

Map of Campo Verano Cemtary:
1. 1867 Campaign Monument
2. Believed location of Julian's Grave

Interested in learning more about the Papal Zouaves?

Than check out Papal Zouave International's other republished books at PapalZouave.com

Or consider becoming a Papal Zouave International member.

Soldier
$30

NCO
$50

- Annual subscription to the *Fidei et Virtuti* Journal Substack
- Assignment of a Papal Zouave to pray for his repose
- Joseph-Louis Guérin prayer cards
- $10 annual coupon for the P.Z.I. store
- A copy of *Adéodat and Emmanuel Dufournel: Officers of the Papal Zouaves*

- All of the perks of the previous tier
- One free P.Z.I. book of your choice annually
- Papal Zouave International lapel pin

Officer
$150

- All of the perks of the previous tier
- Annual print copy of the year's best *Fidei et Virtuti* articles

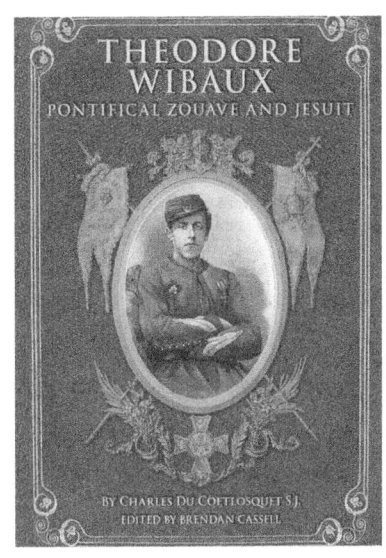

Made in the USA
Coppell, TX
24 February 2026

72298400R00142